Pioneers to Partners

British Aircraft since 1945

Pioneers to Partners
British Aircraft since 1945

Christopher Foyle
& Leo Marriott

CFP

CHRISTOPHER FOYLE PUBLISHING

Glossary

First published in 2009 by
Christopher Foyle Publishing
113-119 Charing Cross Road
London WC2H 0EB

ISBN: 978 0 9548896 1 6

Printed in England by Ian Allan Printing Ltd.

Design: John Shuttleworth.

Acknowledgments

The authors would like to thank the many
who have helped to make this book
possible, by the generous provision of
advice, research, information and
photographs.

Peter Gilchrist for many months of
indefatigable researching of the
photographic archive of BAe Systems
Heritage Centre at Farnborough and the
generous contribution of both his expert
knowledge, writing the captions for the
images in the Research and Development
Aircraft section, liaising with and obtaining
information and images from at least
seventeen museums, collections and BAe
Heritage Centres and generously providing
images from his own collection, Tim
Spearman for many hours, under extreme
time pressure, of the scanning and collation
of the entire collection of photographs, and
of the generous provision of some from his
own collection, Dick Foster for many hours
of research and Hugh Newall Chairman of
the North East Aircraft Museum for
research and frequently providing transport
for Peter Gilchrist in his endeavours, BAe
Heritage Centre at Farnborough namely
Mike Fielding who was most intimately and
energetically involved in seeking out material
and who, sadly, passed away not long
afterwards, Barry Guest, Trevor Friend and
his secretary Wendy Ayling for retrieving
many of the older photographs and guiding
Peter Gilchrist through high mountains of
boxes, BAe Heritage Centre at Brough in
particular Eric Barker and Paul Lawson,
Avro Heritage Centre at Woodford partic-
ularly George Jenks and Harry Holmes,
BAe Systems MR4 Programme at Woodford
namely Ian Lowe and Mark Bolton, BAe
Systems at Warton in particular Dave Ward,
Dave Hutton, Keith Spong and Bob
Fairclough, BAe Systems at Prestwick partic-
ularly Kris Jones, Bristol Aero Collection at
Kemble namely John Battersby and Rex
Canton, International Auster Club in
particular Mick Ames and Mike Preston,
Handley Page Association namely Harry
Fraser-Mitchell, Bombardier Aerospace in
Belfast namely Alan McKight the company
historian, Boulton Paul Association in
particular Les Whitehouse, Miles Aircraft
Collection namely Peter Amos, Agusta-
Westland particularly David Gibbings,
Helicopter Museum at Weston-super-Mare
in particular Elfan ap Rees, Museum of
Berkshire Aviation particularly Ken and Jean
Fosterkew and Tony Vetta, Solent Aviation
Museum in particular Alan Jones, David
Whatley and Alan Mansell, Museum of
Army Flying particularly Susan Lindsay its
Curator, British Airways Museum namely
Paul Jarvis and B.A.'s agency 4-eyes's Bob
Petrie, Strat Mastoris for the image of the
Edgley Optica, Royal Aeronautical Society in
particular Keith Mans its Chief Executive,
Brian Riddle librarian and Chris Male,
Marshall Aerospace at Cambridge partic-
ularly Terry Holloway, Key Publishing Group
namely Richard and Adrian Cox and Paul
Hamblin, RAF Museum in particular Andrew
Renwick the photo librarian, Britten-
Norman Group particularly Stella Work,
John Faulkner, Fleet Air Arm Museum,
Military Aircraft Photos (MAP), Wally Kahn
and Francis Humblet for invaluable advice
and information regarding the list of British
gliders and sailplanes, and Arnold Nayler,
Mike Rentell and Per Lindstrand in respect
of the list of British airships.

We owe particular thanks to Leo McKinstry,
renowned author, journalist and friend, for
coming up with the title "Pioneers to
Partners", denoting the evolution from the
extraordinary independently national
innovation of the 40s, 50s and 60s to the
international cooperative designs of to-day,
resulting in the British aerospace industry
remaining the second largest in the world,
and to Simon Forty of Compendium, our
packager, for many months of essential
editorial and production advice and coordi-
nation of the project.

We are most indebted to His Royal
Highness Prince Philip Duke of Edinburgh
for so generously writing the Foreword.

AAM	Air to Air Missile
ADSM	Air to Surface Missile
AEW	Airborne Early Warning
AFVG	Anglo-French Variable Geometry
AI	Airborne Interception (Radar)
AMRAAM	Advanced Medium Range Air To Air Missile
BA	British Airways (formed in 1973 by merger of BEA and BOAC)
BAC	British Aircraft Corporation
BAe	British Aerospace plc
BEA	British European Airways
BOAC	British Overseas Airways Corporation
EAP	Experimental Aircraft Programme
ESM	Electronic Surveillance Measures
ft	foot (imperial unit of measurement)
FLIR	Forward Looking Infra Red
FTS	Flying Training School
kg	kilogramme (metric unit of weight)
lb st	Pounds Static Thrust (measure of jet engine power output. As a rule of thumb, 1 lb st is approximately equal to 1 hp in a piston engine)
LERX	Leading Edge Root Extensions
LRMTS	Laser Ranging and Market Target Seeker
MAD	Magnetic Anomaly Detector (airborne sensor system for locating submarines)
MDAP	Mutual Defence Assistance Pact
mph	miles per hour
NATO	North Atlantic Treaty Organisation
NVG	Night Vision Goggles
OCU	Operational Conversion Unit
OR	Operational Requirement
RAF	Royal Air Force
RN	Royal Navy
RNAS	Royal Naval Air Station
RWR	Radar Warning Receiver
SACEUR	Strategic Air Command Europe
SBAC	Society of British Aircraft Constructors (now Society of British Aerospace Companies)
STOVL	Short Take Off and Vertical Landing
T&C	Thunder and Colt
TWU	Tactical Weapons Unit
UAV	Unmanned Aerial Vehicle
USMC	United States Marine Corps
VTOL	Vertical Take Off and Landing

Contents

Foreword

By Marshal of the Royal Air Force, HRH The Prince Philip, Duke of Edinburgh, KG, KT.

BUCKINGHAM PALACE.

Before the arrival of the electronic age, aviation was probably the last flowering of the industrial revolution. Stimulated by two world wars, the British aviation industry attracted a remarkable generation of pioneering designers and constructors. They followed in the footsteps of the great British engineers and manufacturers of the 19th and 20th centuries.

The first generation of civil airliners came into service between the wars before immense strides were made in the performance of British military aircraft of all kinds during the second world war. There followed a period of intense development of both military and civil aircraft until the escalating costs of research and development, and the sheer complexities of design and manufacture dictated, first, greater integration of the British aviation industry and then ever wider international partnerships.

This book tells the story of the evolution of the British aviation industry from the immense contribution of the individual pioneers to the invaluable work of the designers and manufacturers of the highly specialised components of contemporary civil and military aircraft. The authors of this book have attempted to illustrate the progress of British aircraft construction since 1945, including the smaller end of the market, where resourceful individuals have made particular contributions. The result is a reminder to everyone of the great pool of engineering and scientific talent which this country possesses.

I was fortunate enough to live through this period, and to have had an unusual opportunity to get to know many of the leaders, and also to fly many of their products. I hope this book will be a reminder of one of the great ages of British engineering initiative, and, hopefully, an inspiration for future engineers.

RIGHT: The Duke of Edinburgh in the cockpit of a Harvard trainer at RAF White Waltham, Berkshire, where he was training for his 'wings'. Prince Philip gained his RAF wings in 1953, his helicopter wings in 1956 and his private pilot's licence in 1959.

BELOW: Prince Philip has been Marshal of the Royal Air Force since 1953.

BOTTOM: Queen Elizabeth II and Prince Philip arriving in Kuwait in February 1979 by Concorde accompanied by then Foreign Secretary Dr David Owen.

Introduction

Although it is only just over 100 years since the Wright Brothers made the first successful flight in a powered aircraft, the aviation industry today plays a vital role in the modern world. The most obvious facet, and the one that impinges most on the ordinary person, is the aircraft as a form of travel. Apart from relatively short distances, anyone contemplating a journey will almost certainly consider an airline flight as their first, and in many cases, only option. This is particularly true in this age of low-cost air fares where even the longest flights, circling half the globe, are within the reach of many people. On the whole, this is a tremendous force for good with people of all races, creeds and nationalities being able to move, meet and mix freely and understand each other better as a consequence. Inevitably, expansion of the air travel industry on such a scale has led to drawbacks and today environmental concerns are being voiced. Regrettably, the high profile of the aviation industry has made it a target for those who would impose their ideals by force and threat rather than by negotiation, and ironically such people are able to communicate better and refine their plans because of their ability to travel freely. Nevertheless, it is difficult to imagine that air travel will not continue to expand and satisfy the basic need and instinct for human travel and communication.

As well as people, a great proportion of the movement of goods and materials around the world is also carried out by air. Commercial airliners carry a considerable amount of general freight in their capacious holds but even so there are many specialist cargo airlines that carry loads of all descriptions, from small, individual parcels to bulk loads of agricultural or commercial goods. Other aviation activities that benefit all of us at one time or another include emergency relief and evacuation, fire-fighting, air ambulances, aerial surveys, law enforcement, and weather-monitoring, to name but a few.

Inevitably, the aeroplane was also seen, from its earliest days, as a weapon of war. As early aircraft were capable of carrying little more than a pilot and perhaps an observer, its offensive capabilities were necessarily limited and the most important application was reconnaissance. This enabled commanders to discover accurately and quickly the disposition of enemy forces and, subsequently, keep them under continuous observation. Obviously, a potential enemy was not going to allow this to happen unhindered and efforts to deny airspace to an opposing force resulted in the first aerial combats and the subsequent development of specialised fighters. As aircraft performance improved they were able to carry increasingly significant loads of military ordnance in the form of bombs, rockets, torpedoes and other devices. This trend culminated in the dropping of two atomic bombs on Japan in August 1945, making the aeroplane the most destructive weapon ever devised by man.

Since 1945 the pace of aeronautical development has increased exponentially as scientific and technical advances have been incorporated at an unbelievable rate. Perhaps the greatest innovation was the jet engine, which became a practical proposition during World War II and was subsequently applied to both military and civil aircraft producing an unimaginable level of improvement in performance. Increasingly, as aerodynamic improvement became incremental by nature, the pace of change was driven by new electronic and digital technologies, which have automated much of the task of actually flying the aircraft and are now involved in their overall operation and interaction with other aircraft and organisations, both on the ground and in the air. Today, it would be entirely possible to produce a pilotless airliner capable of flying efficiently and safely between any two points in the world with its progress tracked and controlled by ground-based and airborne computers (although whether any passenger would be happy with such a set-up is an entirely different question). In terms of technology, another great advance that has been developed since 1945 is the helicopter and other vertical take off aircraft, and these are fulfilling an increasing number of roles in today's world. Finally, of course, aviation technology has been applied to the exploration and exploitation of space outside the world's atmosphere. Increasingly, the benefits of this work is

The English Electric Canberra was one of the best of British postwar designs. It was produced in many variants and remained in RAF service until 2006 – some 57 years after its first flight. There were many export sales and it was built as the B-57 by Martin in the United States.

seen in our everyday lives in the form of satellite communication systems, which are now becoming indispensable, while the miracle of a car-based satellite navigation system is taken totally for granted.

From the earliest days the British aircraft industry has played a central role in all aspects of the advance of aeronautical technology. Although the Wright brothers are credited with the first successful powered flight, there were British pioneers who got close and, some would claim, were actually successful. These included George Cayley, the so-called father of aeronautics, and John Stringfellow, who flew what is claimed to be the first self-powered flying machine at Chard, Somerset, in 1848. Admittedly, this was only a model powered by a small steam engine, but the principle was proved. It was the coming of the internal combustion engine at the closing stages of the 19th century, which was eventually to produce power plants that led ultimately to the Wright brothers' success. Surprisingly, they initially failed to interest the military in their invention and the centre of aviation progress moved to Europe where French pioneers made many advances. This is reflected in the fact that many of the words used to describe the basic parts of an aeroplane (e.g. fuselage, aileron, nacelle) are of French origin. The first powered flight in Britain was made by American-born Samuel Cody in his Aeroplane No.1 at Farnborough on 16 October 1908 and the first all-British flight was by the great pioneer Alliott Verdon Roe in a triplane of his own design on 23 July 1909. The crossing of the English Channel in the same year by Frenchman Louis Bleriot provided both a warning and a stimulus to Britain's fledgling aircraft industry and, as well as Roe, other pioneers such as Geoffrey de Havilland, Tommy Sopwith and Frederick Handley Page designed and flew their own flying machines. Also, in 1909, the famous Short brothers met the Wright brothers on the Isle of Sheppey and concluded an agreement to manufacture the Wright biplanes under licence.

In the face of aircraft development in many other countries, the Aerial League of the British Empire was founded in 1909 by Colonel H. C. Massey and Mr Steven Marples, who saw the need to stimulate the government and the country at large to the emerging importance of aviation for national defence and for commerce. Its warnings were heeded just in time for 1914. It changed its name to the Air League in 1920 and it campaigned in the 1930s for rearmament and also raised money for young men to fly. This was a forerunner of the RAF's Volunteer Reserve Scheme, which was to stand the nation in such good stead when war broke out again in 1939. The Air League founded the Air Defence Cadet Corps in 1938, adopted by the RAF as the Air Training Corps in 1941.

The outbreak of war in 1914 proved to be a watershed for aviation and in the next four years aircraft became much more sophisticated and were produced in their thousands. Many of the famous British aircraft companies were formed at this time and in 1916 their status was underlined by the formation of the Society of British Aircraft Constructors (SBAC) to represent their interests. This organisation remains in existence today although the title has been slightly changed to the Society of British Aerospace Companies to reflect today's interests.

After the armistice in November 1918 the market for military aircraft evaporated virtually overnight and it would take many years for civil aviation to reach the stage where it would support the manufacture of aircraft on any significant scale, especially as the civil demand that did exist could be catered for by the thousands of surplus military aircraft. Inevitably, many of the smaller aircraft constructors went out of business and others were absorbed into some of the larger companies, which themselves were struggling to stay in business. The formation of an independent Royal Air Force (RAF) in 1918 provided at least a trickle of orders and in the 1920s and 1930s steady progress was made so that on the eve of World War II most new aircraft were of all-metal construction and were equipped with devices such as a retractable undercarriage, variable pitch propellers and trailing edge wing flaps. Pilots and crew were accommodated in enclosed cockpits or flight decks. On the whole, the British Air Ministry preferred the use of liquid cooled in-line engines and experience with the Schneider Trophy seaplane races was incorporated by Rolls-Royce into their new PV-12 engine, better known as the Merlin. Initially rated at around 1,000 hp, this was progressively increased to around 1,800 hp in later versions. This engine went on to power almost all the famous British wartime aircraft such as the Spitfire, Hurricane, Mosquito and Lancaster. A scaled-up version known as the Griffon produced over 2,000 hp and was used in many post-war designs. While Rolls-Royce concentrated on the Merlin and its derivatives, the Bristol Aero Engine Company held faith with the air-cooled radial engine resulting in the Hercules, which notably powered the Bristol Beaufighter and Handley Page Halifax. Subsequently they produced the Centaurus, which produced over 2,500 hp and powered the last generations of British piston-engined fighters, the Hawker Tempest II and Sea Fury.

The resurgence of the British aircraft industry began in the mid-1930s when the threat posed by Nazi Germany could no longer be ignored and preparations for war began in earnest. The sudden demand for large numbers of aircraft meant that individual aircraft companies could not fulfil orders from their own resources and it was often necessary to arrange subcontractors. This inevitably led to some degree of rationalisation and although individual company names and design bureaux were retained, they were often part of a greater organisation. Typical of this was the Hawker Siddeley merger, which itself came about by the merging of Hawker Aircraft and the Armstrong Siddeley group in 1935. Prior to that, Hawkers had already taken over the Gloster Aircraft Company in 1935 and the Armstrong Siddeley group had taken over A.V. Roe in 1928. The other big players were the Bristol Aeroplane Company with its Bristol Aero Engine subsidiary, and Vickers, which had taken over the engineering interests of Armstrong Whitworth and had also acquired Southampton-based Supermarine Aviation, both in 1928. There was also de Havilland, which, like Bristol, had its own substantial aero engine division. Other major independent companies included Handley Page, Short Brothers and Westland. Even so, the demands of war production led to the creation of numerous shadow factories that drew their management and labour force from other sectors, notably the motor and furniture industries.

When peace came in 1945, there was obviously a massive contraction of the British aircraft industry but, for various reasons, it was not as severe as that experienced in 1918. For a start, much of the surplus manufacturing capacity was lost by closing down the shadow factories or converting them to production of other essential goods in the post-war era (prefabricated housing being a typical example). Also it was only three years before the onset of the Cold War, heralded by the Soviet blockade of Berlin and the subsequent successful allied airlift. This led ultimately to the formation of the North Atlantic Treaty Organisation (NATO) but this was preceded by the United States (US)-financed Marshall Plan and the Mutual Defence Assistance Pact (MDAP), which provided funds for the rebuilding of the European nations devastated by war and allowed them to re-equip their air forces. The demand for military aircraft was heightened by the fact that the jet engine had made piston-engined combat aircraft obsolete virtually overnight and, consequently, even the RAF, which had substantial numbers of conventional aircraft available, was forced into an expensive re-equipment programme. These efforts received a massive boost with the outbreak of the Korean War in 1951 and a number of aircraft such as the Hawker Hunter, Supermarine Swift and English Electric Canberra were rushed into production under a 'Super Priority' programme.

Even on the civil side, prospects were much brighter than in 1918. In the years immediately preceding World War II, civil aviation was just beginning to establish itself as a reliable means of transport with the introduction of new all metal twin- or four-engined airliners led, of course, by the American Douglas DC-3. However, the outbreak of war in 1939 led to an almost total cessation of the development of British civil transport aircraft so that by 1945 the Americans had achieved a commanding lead with modern types of aircraft such as the Douglas DC-4 and the Lockheed Constellation already in service and derivatives such as the DC-6, Super Constellation and Boeing Stratocruiser all just around the corner. Faced with this situation, the British had already had recourse to their favourite reaction to any crisis – they set up a committee! This was the eponymous Brabazon Committee, which was set up in 1943 under the chairmanship of Lord Brabazon with a directive to investigate the types of civil aircraft that would be required in the post-war years and to frame outline

specifications for each type. Their work was to have a far-reaching effect on the types of aircraft produced by the British aircraft industry, not all of it beneficial, and it is relevant to consider the Committee's recommendations outlining five basic aircraft types:

• Brabazon Type I was to be a large airliner capable of operating non-stop in both directions on the important London–New York route and carrying passengers in considerable luxury.

• Type II was seen as a feeder liner that would supplant the DC-3 and de Havilland Dragon Rapide. However, input from BEA resulted in two later specifications, a Type IIA for a larger piston-engined airliner and Type IIB, which was similar but would be powered by the new turboprop engines.

• Type III called for a 32-seat transport capable of covering 2,500 miles at a cruising speed of 300mph.

• Type IV was a more revolutionary concept, calling for a jet-powered airliner and this was included mainly at the instigation of Geoffrey de Havilland.

• Type V was a revised specification for a small feeder liner to replace the de Havilland Rapide after the original Type II specification had been altered to produce much larger aircraft.

The first of these led to the mighty Bristol Brabazon, the largest airliner ever built at the time of its maiden flight in September 1949 and a distinction it maintained until the Boeing 747 flew some 20 years later. Unfortunately, a combination of technical difficulties and political attitudes meant that only the prototype was flown and the Brabazon never entered service. More successful was the Type II specification that led to the graceful twin-engined Airspeed Ambassador. However this was a conventional piston-engined aircraft but an offshoot from the Type II specification indirectly led to the Vickers Viscount, one of the great success stories of the post-war aircraft industry. Although in its initial production form seating capacity started at around 40–50 seats, this rose to 70–80 in later variants, much in excess of the 24 passengers originally envisaged. The rival Armstrong Whitworth Apollo powered by four Mamba turboprops was less successful and only two prototypes were completed. In the meantime the Type III specification produced few viable

contenders but eventually formed the basis of work that led to the Bristol Britannia.

The Type IV specification resulted in the airliner that promised to give Britain an unassailable lead in the production of civil airliners. This was the revolutionary de Havilland Comet, the world's first jet airliner, which flew in July 1949 and initially proved to be an outstanding success with passengers. So much so that orders began to pour in from airlines around the world but the early promise was shattered by a series of fatal crashes that led to the Comet being grounded while extensive tests were carried out to determine the cause and to allow the necessary redesign to take place. By the time the definitive Comet IV was ready for service, Boeing had caught up with their 707 jet airliner based on the original Model 387-80 that had flown in 1954. Although the British Overseas Airways Corporation (BOAC) Comets gained the distinction of operating the first jet transatlantic scheduled flights in 1958, the Boeing 707, together with the Douglas DC-8 swept the market. Finally the Type V specification was split into a Type VA and VB, the former resulting in the four-engined Miles Marathon and the latter led to the twin-engined de Havilland Dove.

What might have been achieved if the aircraft manufacturers had been left to produce aircraft based solely on their own commercial instincts is illustrated by the highly successful Avro 748 (later to become the Hawker Siddeley/ BAe 748). This rugged twin-engined turboprop airliner flew in 1960 and over 380 were eventually produced, including 160 built under licence in India. A rival design was the Aviation Traders Accountant. This actually pre-dated the Avro 748, having flown in prototype form in 1957 but no production orders were forthcoming. Although superficially similar, the Avro 748 was a much more advanced aircraft from a technical point of view (it was the first airliner designed with a fail-safe structure) and, crucially, it carried twice as many passengers.

Inevitably aircraft, both military and civil, grew more complex and expensive as the decades passed. The end of the Korean War slowed down the demand for military aircraft and the notorious 1957 Defence White Paper, forecasting the end of manned military aircraft, was not helpful. In fact, as a concept, it was not perhaps as extreme as it seemed at the time given the progress of today's unmanned aerial vehicles (UAVs) but in 1957 the technology was not in place. Also, despite the success of the Viscount, the British industry was struggling to compete with American manufacturers and it was obvious that some form of consolidation was inevitable. This came about in 1960 when the Hawker Siddeley Group finally brought all of its constituent aircraft manufacturing companies under one organisation, Hawker Siddeley Aircraft Ltd. This spelt the end of many famous names such as Avro whose Vulcan bomber now became the Hawker Siddeley Vulcan, and Armstrong Whitworth, whose Argosy transport was now the Hawker Siddeley Argosy. At the same time the de Havilland Company was absorbed into the Hawker Siddeley Group and lost its own identity. The other major aircraft construction group was the British Aircraft Corporation (BAC), which officially came into being in 1963 following earlier amalgamations among its constituent companies starting with Vickers, the Bristol Aircraft Company and English Electric in 1960. This group then absorbed Hunting Aircraft Ltd, which itself had been formed by the take over of Percival Aircraft. Other consolidations included Fairey Aviation, producers of naval aircraft and helicopters, who were taken over by Westland in 1958, while as far back as 1948 Handley Page took over the assets of Miles Aircraft at Woodley.

The new conglomerates had to fight hard for what few military orders were available. The Hawker Siddeley Group had inherited the revolutionary P.1127 vertical take off project, which had first flown in 1960 and was eventually developed into the famous Harrier and Sea Harrier STOVL (Short Take Off and Vertical Landing) fighters. A more ambitious project was the supersonic P.1154 but this was cancelled in 1964 by the incoming Wilson Government, one of three major projects axed at that time in what was something of a watershed for the British aircraft industry. One of these was the BAC TSR.2 supersonic strike bomber, which had first flown on 27 September 1964 and, subsequently, had demonstrated great promise. In terms of performance, it was potentially a world beater and certainly the Americans had nothing to match it at the time. Nevertheless, the TSR.2 was sacrificed at the altar of political dogma and the programme was cancelled

in April 1965. The government was so determined that the project should never be re-instated at a later date that it ordered all the production jigs to be broken up. The third cancelled project was the vertical take off Armstrong Whitworth 681 four-engined tactical transport.

On the civil side Vickers had already produced the graceful VC-10, probably the best looking jet airliner ever built and one that in its Super VC-10 version was superior to the Boeing 707 on several counts. Nevertheless, it was very late to the market and sales were disappointing although it did have a second life as a military transport and tanker. BAC on the other hand had more success with the One Eleven, a jet airliner, with twin rear-mounted engines and a T-tail. Unfortunately, it fell victim to the usual British problem of being in advance of other nations and the prototype crashed after experiencing the hitherto unrecognised phenomena of a super stall. The problem was diagnosed quickly and remedial modifications were incorporated in the second prototype. Subsequently, over 200 One Elevens were sold – a significant achievement by British standards but not so against the almost 1,000 Douglas DC-9s that flew after the BAC-111, and that were able to benefit from the British experience.

Another market leader! The Vickers Viscount was the world's first turboprop airliner to fly and entered service in 1950. It was retired by British Airways in 1985 but continued in service in small numbers well into the 21st century.

The ultimate airliner was the supersonic Concorde, whose development was initiated by the same Labour Government that had cancelled the round of military aircraft. The Concorde was, of course, an international Anglo-French project and the British prototype flew in 1969. Although a great technical success, Concorde did not achieve any true commercial success. Very few were built but it did show that the way forward for the British aircraft industry was in international collaboration and this resulted in the abortive Anglo-French Variable Geometry (AFVG) strike aircraft project. However, this led in turn to the Panavia Tornado, which was built by a tri-nation consortium from Britain, Germany and Italy. Anglo-French relations thrived on the Jaguar twin-jet fighter and resulted in a helicopter deal, whereby British and French armed forces received Puma, Gazelle and Lynx helicopters, the latter designed and built by Westland.

All this was accomplished against a further consolidation and contraction of the industry. One of the great names, Handley Page, went into receivership in

The partnership between Aérospatiale and BAC led to the world's most beautiful aircraft – the Concorde supersonic transport. It served for 27 years, regularly crossed the Atlantic in around three hours and could always be counted on to be a show-stopper wherever it was seen.

1969, although production of its successful Jetstream light turboprop transport was transferred to Scottish Aviation at Prestwick. A much more significant event was the formation of British Aerospace (BAe) in 1977, which was achieved by the merging of BAC and the Hawker Siddeley Group, as well as rounding up Scottish Aviation and other smaller concerns. In this form BAe became virtually the only major airframe manufacturer, apart from Westland, which concentrated solely on helicopters. Over the years the number of British-designed aircraft in production has dwindled, with the only current programmes being the Hawk jet trainer and the Nimrod maritime patrol aircraft. On the other hand, BAe was a substantial partner in the design and production of the Tornado multi-role aircraft and today, as BAE Systems is also a major partner in the Eurofighter Typhoon programme. In addition, it has numerous links with US companies and is a major subcontractor to several major projects. Until 2007 it was also a major partner in Airbus, a position inherited from Hawker Siddeley, but sold out to Airbus in that year in order to raise

capital for other investments. BAe did actually produce one jet airliner, the British Aerospace 146 later rebranded as the Avro RJ series, which in terms of sales was the most successful British jet airliner selling over 350 aircraft. A foray into a complementary turboprop resulted in the BAe ATP which was based on the earlier Avro/BAe 748. However it failed to achieve the sales of its predecessor and only 67 were completed.

In joining the original Airbus consortium Hawker Siddeley ensured that British factories at Bristol and Chester became centres of excellence in the design and manufacture of wings using advanced techniques and modern composite materials. Despite their sale to Airbus in 2007, these British centres remain a vital part of the whole Airbus organisation (the Bristol centre has in turn been sold to GKN, a British company with wide aerospace interests). In addition, many Airbus aircraft are powered by Rolls-Royce engines while other British concerns supply a significant proportion of the myriad systems and components which go to make up a modern airliner. Consequently, although no Airbus final assembly line has have been set up in the United Kingdom (UK), the authors have no doubt that the various Airbus products should feature in this book.

Apart from major military and civil projects, Britain also had a good

reputation for building graceful and efficient light aircraft. In the post-war era the main names were Miles, Percival, Auster and de Havilland. However, financial constraints and growing American competition virtually killed off this aspect of aircraft production in the post-war decades. As already stated, Miles Aircraft was taken over by Handley Page in 1948 while Percival became part of the Hunting Group in 1944 forming Hunting Percival Aircraft, which itself was absorbed by BAC in 1960. Perhaps the most prolific was Auster, which survived until 1960 when it became part of Beagle (British Executive and General Aviation Ltd). Although this company produced some interesting aircraft, including the much liked Beagle Pup trainer, it went into liquidation in 1970. In the post-war years de Havilland produced the successful Dove and Heron but a successor to the famous Tiger Moth was the Canadian-designed Chipmunk. A successful enterprise was Britten Norman, which produced the twin-engined Islander in 1965. Despite world wide sales success, the company did not thrive and has been bought and sold many times although the Islander remains in production today.

This book attempts to tell the story of the post-war British aircraft industry by briefly describing every aircraft designed and built in Britain since 1945. As a starting point it will include all aircraft of which the first prototype, or prototype of a major new variant made its first flight on or after 1 January 1945. For the sake of completeness it will also include the various international programmes either where the resulting aircraft was built in the United Kingdom (UK) (e.g. Tornado) or where significant components were manufactured in the UK (e.g. Airbus or Joint Strike Fighter). Foreign-designed aircraft, which were actually built and produced in the UK (e.g. various Westland helicopters) are also included. For ease of reference, the aircraft are dealt with under the categories listed in the contents page and within these sections aircraft are arranged by date of first flight.

1 Military Aircraft

Jet Aircraft

At the end of World War II the British aircraft industry was already deeply involved in the development of jet combat aircraft with the Meteor twin jet fighter already in squadron service and the new twin-boom Vampire just beginning to reach operational units. In addition, the aero engine industry, building on the pioneering work of Sir Frank Whittle, was the world leader in matters of jet propulsion with companies such as Rolls Royce, Armstrong Siddeley and de Havilland producing engines that offered not only ever increasing thrust ratings but also a degree of reliability that did much to further the acceptance of this still revolutionary form of propulsion. Of course, in many ways, the British aircraft industry had not been as advanced as that of Germany but with the latter's defeat the fruits of the country's research became available as technical missions brought back priceless information and even, sometimes, whole aircraft.

Initially, this treasure trove had little effect as the development of the basic Meteor and Vampire designs continued and variants formed the front-line strength of not only the Royal Air Force but also many Commonwealth and European air arms. The Meteor, originally intended as a single-seat day fighter, evolved into a two-seat radar-equipped night fighter. Dedicated trainer and photographic reconnaissance versions were produced. Specially prepared examples captured the World Speed Record in November 1945 and again in September 1946. The Vampire was also widely exported and was also produced in two-seat trainer and night-fighter versions. A new wing with a swept back leading edge resulted in the Venom, which had a much improved performance and, again, this aircraft achieved major export successes.

Perhaps the most outstanding British jet aircraft of the post-war era was the twin-engined Canberra bomber, which first flew in 1949 and was the best light bomber of the next three decades, a few examples still remaining in service today. The Canberra was notable as being one of the few foreign combat aircraft ever to be produced under licence in the US – a reversal of what was to become normal procedure. However, the Canberra shared one feature in common with the Meteor and Vampire in that its design incorporated a straight wing. Analysis of German experience clearly showed the benefits of sweepback and although some prototypes were flown, it was the Americans and Russians who were quickest off the mark with the immortal Sabre and the equally famous Mig-15 (even if the latter was powered by an

The Gloster Meteor flew operationally from 1944 to 1965. The first Allied jet to see action in World War II, it also saw combat during the Korean and Arab-Israeli wars. This is the NF.11 night fighter variant – see page 38.

engine of British design!). Both these aircraft were in service at the outbreak of the Korean War but the first British swept wing fighter, the beautiful Hawker Hunter, did not enter service until 1954.

In the mid to late 1950s the RAF began to receive the trio of V-bombers that were to provide the nuclear deterrent force until this role passed to the Polaris missile submarines of the Royal Navy (RN) in 1967. Of these the Vulcan was perhaps the best all rounder with a fighter-like performance at high altitudes due to its delta wing, although the contemporary Victor could carry a heavier bomb-load. The continued development of British jet combat aircraft received a major setback in the misguided 1957 Defence White Paper that forecast the end of manned aircraft and caused the cancellation of several promising projects. The only one to survive was the English Electric Lightning, which was to become the only wholly British combat aircraft capable of exceeding the speed of sound (Mach 1) in level flight. Conceived as a pure interceptor it had a startling performance but was restricted by limited endurance.

The 1957 setback was almost insignificant compared with the damage inflicted on the British aircraft industry by the Wilson Government in 1964/65 when it cancelled the TSR.2 advanced strike bomber and the Hawker Siddeley P.1154 supersonic Vertical Take Off and Landing (VTOL) fighter. With these flagship projects swept away, the industry was forced into the path of international collaboration, which today is perhaps the only way in which the continually spiralling cost of producing sophisticated combat aircraft can be met. Thus after the abortive AFVG strike aircraft, the Panavia Tornado was born.

At the same time Anglo-French cooperation resulted in the Jaguar single-seat fighter, while today the multi-nation Eurofighter consortium is producing the Typhoon multi-role fighter at various establishments including BAE Systems at Warton in Lancashire. The latter company continues to produce the last indigenous military jet in the shape of the Hawk trainer, which first flew in 1974 and continues to sell – its success perhaps influenced by its exposure as the mount of the famous Red Arrows.

ABOVE: The Harrier GR.7 first flew in May 1990 and became the RAF's standard model. It was deployed operationally for the first time over former Yugslavia in August 1995.

ABOVE RIGHT: The Hawker Sea Fury was the Fleet Air Arm's primary fighter-bomber during the early 1950s..

BELOW RIGHT: The RAF's basic trainer, the Tucano, is built under license by Shorts.

BAe Systems, and its predecessor Hawker Siddeley, have been responsible for one of the great advances in military aircraft – the successful development of the vertical take off Harrier family. Evolved from the earlier P1127 and Kestrel, the Harrier is the only successful aircraft of its type and, like the Canberra, has been adopted eagerly by US forces. In fact, production of the latest Harrier versions is now centred in America with BAE Systems being a major subcontractor. This situation is echoed by the next family of jet combat aircraft, the Joint Strike Fighter, which will enter service during the next decade and assures the British aerospace industry of a continuing place at the top table.

Propeller-driven Aircraft

Despite the advent of the jet engine, there was a continued demand for propeller-driven aircraft to perform a variety of military roles. Many of these were the final iterations of famous World War II aircraft such as the Spitfire, which was still in production after 1945 with advanced versions being delivered to the RAF and RN in 1948 and 1949, respectively. Britain's last front-line piston-engined fighter was the Hawker Sea Fury, which first flew in 1945 and was in production until 1952. Its companion on carrier flight decks was the elegant Fairey Firefly, which was produced to carry out a variety of roles including fighter reconnaissance and anti-submarine patrol. The torpedo strike role was carried out by Blackburn Firebrands, which were in service from 1945 to 1953. Both the Firefly and the Firebrand were eventually replaced by turboprop aircraft, the former by the unique twin Mamba powered Fairey Gannet and the latter by the Westland Wyvern. The Wyvern was one aircraft that typified much of the British aircraft industry's problems at the time – it was many years in development with testing dogged by unreliable power-plants and was already obsolescent when it eventually entered service in 1953. For a few years after the war, twin-piston-engined aircraft such as the Mosquito, Hornet and Sea Hornet and Bristol Brigand carried out front-line roles until they too were replaced by more advanced jets.

During World War II the backbone of the bomber force were the four-engined heavies such as the Halifax and Lancaster, and after 1945 the Avro Lincoln entered service. However, the future lay with the new jet bombers of which the Canberra was the outstanding example but the Lancaster heritage lived on in the Avro Shackleton maritime patrol aircraft. First flown in 1949, the final Airborne Early Warning (AEW) variant was still in service as late as 1991, testimony to the protracted wrangles over the development of a successor platform rather than the venerable aircraft's suitability for the role in the late 20th century!

Propeller-driven aircraft retained a role in training military aircrew even to the present day but in the post-war era a number of aircraft in this category were produced. Perhaps the most successful was the de Havilland Chipmunk (admittedly designed in Canada!) but

others included the Prentice, Provost and Bulldog for basic training and the more advanced Balliol for advanced training. In due course some of these were replaced by jets but today the RAF's basic trainer is the turboprop Tucano, a Brazilian design built under licence in Northern Ireland by Shorts, and early pilot grading and elementary training is carried out in light-piston-engined aircraft such as the Slingsby T67 and the imported Grob Tutor.

In 1957 the Army Air Corps was formed and this organisation inherited

several AOP squadrons from the RAF, almost exclusively equipped with Auster AOP.6s although these were replaced by the more powerful and updated AOP.9. Earlier attempts to produce a dedicated spotter aircraft resulted in the Heston AOP prototype, which did not enter production.

There were, of course, several civil airliners and transports that were either converted or produced for military use and these are described in Part 2.

Supermarine Spiteful 8 January 1945

Hawker Sea Fury 21 January 1945

Gloster Meteor F. Mk. 4 12 April 1945

LEFT: The Supermarine Type 371 Spiteful was a direct development of the Spitfire, comprising a standard Spitfire Mk. 14 fitted with a more efficient laminar-flow wing. As the design progressed, the fuselage and tail structures were also redesigned, ultimately producing a completely new aircraft. The first Spiteful made its maiden flight on 30 June 1944. Powered by a 2,035hp Griffon engine and armed with four 20mm cannon, the Spiteful had great potential – it achieved the fastest speed of any British piston-engined aircraft, 494mph, in 1947 – and a batch of 188 was ordered. The end of hostilities, and developments in jet-engine technology, led to the order being cancelled and only 19 aircraft were completed. Later versions of the Spiteful (none saw service) included the F.5 with a six-bladed contra-rotating prop.

BELOW LEFT: The Hawker Sea Fury was the Fleet Air Arm's primary fighter-bomber during the early 1950s. Developed initially from a light fighter design for the RAF, it was destined to replace the Tempest and Typhoon. RAF interest was abandoned at the end of World War II, but the naval derivative was pursued and more than 800 Sea Furies were eventually produced and it saw action with the FAA and Australian Navy during the Korean War. The Sea Fury was one of the fastest piston-engined machines ever produced, capable of reaching speeds of 480kts.

ABOVE RIGHT: The Meteor F. Mk. 4 fighter entered production in 1946. Derived from earlier Meteor designs, it featured clipped-span wings, a pair of Derwent 5 engines in redesigned nacelles, a strengthened airframe, a fully pressurised cockpit and improved ailerons and rudder trim. In comparison to the original Meteor Mk. 1's top speed of 415mph, the F.4 could achieve 585mph. Many of the initial deliveries went to export customers, and eventually a total of 13 RAF Squadrons re-equipped with the type, with some 535 aircraft being manufactured for the RAF. The Meteor twin-seat dual-control variant was also developed from the F.4 airframe.

RIGHT: Based on the Mosquito, de Havilland's Hornet was a faster and more manoeuvrable design which took advantage of developments in laminar-flow wing design, airframe refinements and engine development. Retaining much of the Mosquito's wooden construction, the Hornet was equipped with streamlined engines and outwards-turning propellers. The Sea Hornet F.20 (of which 79 were produced) entered service with the FAA in 1947. A further 72 aircraft were produced to NF.21 night fighter standard, equipped with a second cockpit, exhaust flame dampers and radar. The Sea Hornet PR.22 was a specialised PR variant: 23 were built with three cameras installed in the rear fuselage. Although largely replaced in FAA service by the Sea Fury, the Sea Hornet remained in active use through the mid-1950s.

De Havilland Sea Hornet 19 April 1945

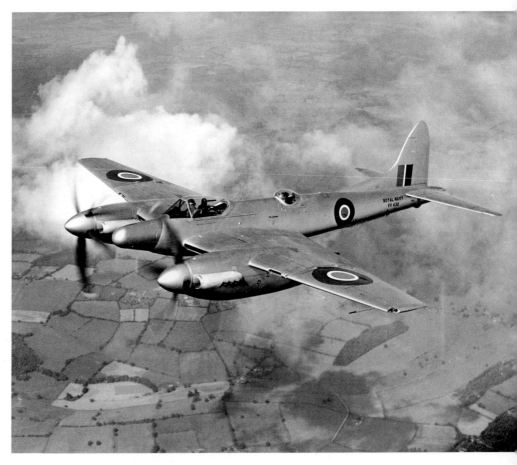

De Havilland Vampire F. Mk. 1 20 April 1945

Auster AOP.6 1 May 1945

Blackburn Firebrand TF Mk. 4 17 May 1945

ABOVE LEFT: The de Havilland DH.100 was one of the two early post-war fighter designs (the other was the Meteor) which Britain developed around the then-new jet engine. Initially named 'Spider Crab', the aircraft emerged as the Vampire F. 1, a simple design created around a single centrifugal-flow Goblin engine. Taking advantage of de Havilland's expertise in metal and moulded plywood construction, the Vampire F. 1 featured a twin-boom tail design which eliminated the need for a long engine exhaust which would have reduced power output. As it was, the Vampire F. 1 still lacked significant power and range. The first production aircraft took to the air in April 1945 and although the aircraft would have been invaluable for combat operations, the type did not enter RAF service until after World War II, some 244 aircraft being manufactured after which production shifted to the more powerful Mk. 3 and Mk. 5 aircraft which became the RAF's main fighter-bomber type into the 1950s. A naval derivative of the Vampire F.1 made the world's first jet launch and recovery from an aircraft carrier on 3 December 1945.

BELOW LEFT: Designed as a development of the Taylorcraft Auster V, the Auster AOP.6 featured a strengthened fuselage, external fixed aerofoil flaps and lengthened undercarriage struts to accommodate a larger propeller, powered by a 145hp Gipsy Major 7 engine. Entering service in the late 1940s the aircraft was used extensively by the RAF (who received 312 aircraft) and the Army Air Corps as an air observation and light communications aircraft. With a useful short-field take off capability and excellent reliability, the AOP.6 was an invaluable part of post-war British military operations, seeing service in both Korea and Malaya. More than 400 aircraft were produced with exports being made to Australia, Belgium, Burma, Canada, Hong Kong, India, Jordan, New Zealand and South Africa, some of these aircraft being dual-control variants (the AOP.7). The aircraft was gradually replaced by the more capable AOP.9 from 1955 onwards and many aircraft were refurbished for civilian use, some still being in regular use today.

ABOVE: The Blackburn Firebrand TF. 4 was the first main production variant of Blackburn's less-than-successful strike-fighter. Originally designed as a twin-seat interceptor, changing requirements eventually saw the aircraft emerge as a single-seat fighter which first flew in February 1942. Although small numbers of Napier Sabre-engined Firebrands were produced, it was the Centaurus IX-powered Mk. 5 which became the major production variant – some 102 aircraft being built, equipped with both larger tail surfaces (to counter the increased torque of the larger engine) and dive brakes, enabling the Firebrand to deliver successfully a single fuselage-mounted torpedo. However, the Firebrand's performance was unremarkable (a top speed of 350mph) and with the cockpit positioned closer to the tail than the nose, visibility for the pilot was poor. Perhaps the most interesting aspect of the Firebrand's design was the installation of an externally mounted airspeed gauge which enabled the pilot to keep his eyes outside of the cockpit during deck landings – the forerunner of today's head-up displays.

Miles Monitor Autumn 1945

Percival Prentice 31 March 1946

ABOVE: The Miles Monitor was created in response to an RAF need for a high-speed target tug with a top speed of at least 300mph and an endurance of 3–4 hours. Eventually the RAF's interest waned, but the FAA needed an aircraft to simulate dive attacks on ships for fleet training purposes and the Monitor was developed further to incorporate dive brakes and radar for accurate measurement of altitude – useful for fleet gunnery practice. As World War II ended, an order for 600 was cancelled and only 20 were built, these being used for evaluation purposes, mostly at Boscombe Down.

LEFT: Created in response to an RAF requirement for a Tiger Moth and Harvard replacement, the Prentice was the first all-metal aircraft to be constructed by Percival. More than 370 aircraft were delivered to the RAF between 1947 and 1949. Designed as a basic trainer, the aircraft carried an instructor and a student, with a second student in a rear seat to gain air experience. The Prentice was sturdy but with sluggish handling and little power. It was regarded as a stop-gap trainer which was rapidly replaced by the Chipmunk and Provost, the final training flights taking place in 1953. Many of the former RAF machines were bought for civilian conversion. Some 66 aircraft were manufactured under licence for the Indian Air Force (as illustrated) and although a small number of aircraft have survived both in the UK and elsewhere, only one remains airworthy.

Miles M.37 Martinet Trainer 11 April 1946

LEFT: The Miles M.25 Martinet was the first British aircraft designed as a target tug. Based on the Miles Master, the design featured a revised cockpit position, a longer nose and increased wing span, plus a strengthened structure capable of handling the stresses created by target towing. The targets and associated gear were housed in a fairing under the fuselage. The Martinet's first flight took place on 24 April 1942 and a total of 1,724 aircraft were produced primarily for the RAF and FAA. The M.50 Queen Martinet was an unmanned radio-controlled drone derivative, whilst the M.37 was a twin-seat conversion trainer (only two were manufactured).

BELOW: Originally designed as a carrier-borne torpedo bomber, at the end of World War II the Short SA.1 Sturgeon was redesigned as a PR aircraft. The Sturgeon PR.1 reached prototype stage (first flying in June 1946) but the order for 100 aircraft was cancelled. Re-emerging as a target tug, the Sturgeon TT.2 reached the production stage and entered service with the FAA. Of the 24 aircraft manufactured, five were later converted to a TT.3 standard during the early 1950s. The final variant of the Sturgeon was the SB.3 designed to meet a requirement for an anti-submarine warfare aircraft for the FAA.

Short Sturgeon 7 June 1946

Supermarine Seafang F. Mk. 32 30 June 1946

ABOVE: The Supermarine Type 383 Seafang was a direct development of the Spiteful, destined for naval use. Equipped with the same laminar-flow wing as the Spiteful, the aircraft was redesigned for carrier operations. The Seafang F.31 (ten manufactured) was the first variant, fitted with a five-bladed propeller powered by a Griffon 61 engine, however the later Mk. 32 was a more refined design better suited to FAA operations, complete with tail hook, folding wings, increased fuel capacity and a 2,350hp Griffon 89 engine driving contra-rotating propellers (which eliminated torque). Some 18 Seafangs were eventually produced but not all of these reached flight status and those that did (only 11 in all) were used purely for design and development work and the aircraft never entered operational service. Although the Seafang performed well during trials (including deck landings and launches) its performance was not sufficiently impressive to compete with emerging naval derivatives of the jet-powered Meteor and Vampire and as such, the Seafang undoubtedly represented the very end of the Spitfire's design potential, although its wing design did survive into the jet age and was used by the Attacker.

ABOVE RIGHT: Designed as a successor to the Fulmar, the Firefly made its first flight on 22 December 1941. Significantly heavier than its predecessor, the Firefly was some 40mph faster, thanks to a powerful (1,735hp) Griffon engine. Armed with a pair of 20mm cannon in each wing, the Firefly Mk. 1 was a hugely successful design of which some 200 aircraft were ordered. This variant became the most widely used version of the Firefly during World War II. The first aircraft was delivered in 1943 and entered operational service the following year. The aircraft was used in a variety of theatres including Europe (where the aircraft was also used for armed reconnaissance and anti-shipping strikes) and Fireflies provided air cover for the strike on the Tirpitz in 1944. In the Far East, the Firefly was the first British-built and designed aircraft to fly over Tokyo. Many Firefly variants were developed, including a number of dual-control trainer variants (as illustrated) which featured a second raised cockpit towards the rear of the fuselage. The T.1 was a direct trainer development of the Mk. 1 fighter, whilst the T.2 was an armed operational training aircraft based on the same airframe.

Fairey Firefly Trainer July 1946

Supermarine Attacker 27 July 1946

RIGHT: The first jet aircraft ever produced by Supermarine was the Type 392, that flew on 27 July 1946. The second prototype (TS413) flew on 17 June 1947, at which time the aircraft officially became the Attacker F.1 – the RN's first jet fighter. A total of 183 Attackers was built with some 36 aircraft being sold to Pakistan. Initially referred to as the 'Jet Spiteful' the Attacker was a direct jet-powered development of the Spiteful, retaining the same laminar-flow wing. Unfortunately it also retained the same tail-wheel undercarriage which led to difficulties, not least during deck landings and the risk of considerable damage to paved and grass-covered landing strips (which were inevitably damaged by the Attacker's low-mounted jet exhaust). The Attacker was produced in three variants: the F.1 fighter which entered service in 1951 (armed with four 20mm cannon), the FB.1 fighter-bomber derivative, and the FB.2 which featured an improved Nene engine and strengthened airframe which enabled the aircraft to carry a greater variety of external stores. The Attacker was withdrawn from front line duties in 1954 but remained in use with the Royal Naval Volunteer Reserve until 1956.

Westland Wyvern (Eagle engine) 12 December 1946

Blackburn B.48 (YA.1) 1 April 1947

ABOVE: Produced in response to the need for a long-range carrier- or land-based fighter, Westland's W34 design became the Wyvern. Its most striking features were the high-mounted cockpit and the huge contra-rotating propellers, designed to minimise their diameter and eliminate torque swing – important considerations for deck operations. The Wyvern's difficulties mainly surrounded the engine. The prototype was powered by a monstrous 3,450hp Rolls-Royce Eagle – the manufacturer's largest and most powerful (and last) piston engine. The Eagle engine was relatively new and difficulties quickly arose. After RAF interest in the programme was abandoned, official support for further piston engine development waned, and Westland opted to re-engine with a turboprop.

LEFT: The Blackburn YA.1 (later named Firecrest) was a development of the Firebrand. The YA.1 emerged with a more practical design. The cockpit and canopy had been brought forward along the fuselage; the new inverted-gull wings featured four Fowler flaps which gave the aircraft a much better landing performance and retractable flaps were included to equip the aircraft for the strike role. However, rapid advances were being made with jet- and turboprop-powered designs and the Firecrest's performance was insufficiently advanced to justify purchase by the FAA. Consequently, although three prototypes were built, the aircraft was abandoned in 1948.

Boulton Paul Balliol (Merlin engine)

10 July 1947

LEFT AND BELOW: Boulton Paul's Balliol was designed to meet an RAF requirement for a three-seat advanced trainer capable of replacing the ageing fleet of Harvards. It was envisaged that it would be powered by the then-new turboprop engine (an Armstrong Siddeley Mamba), but development was slow and the prototype Balliol was fitted with a Bristol Mercury radial engine (as illustrated), taking to the air for the first time on 30 May 1947. Following a change in RAF requirements, the Balliol was redesigned as a twin-seat advanced trainer, powered by a Rolls-Royce Merlin. It was in this form (the T.2) that the aircraft entered RAF service in 1950 and although the turboprop-powered T.1 did not proceed beyond prototype status, the piston-engined T.2 was successful, its career cut short by the RAF's interest in all-jet advanced training. Naval interest in the aircraft resulted in the Sea Balliol T.21, also powered by a Merlin but equipped with a tail hook and folding wings. Twelve aircraft were also exported to the Royal Ceylon Air Force.

Hawker Sea Fury Trainer 15 January 1948

ABOVE: The single-seat Sea Fury FB.11 became famous as the FAA's stalwart fighter-bomber during the 1950s. It was also produced as a dual-control variant, designated Sea Fury T. Mk. XX. The aircraft (prototype illustrated) was identical to the single-seat FB.11 but a second cockpit was installed, complete with a full set of flying controls and instruments. Minor changes were made to the aircraft's tailplanes and rudder, and two of the wing-mounted machine guns were replaced by oxygen equipment. In all other respects the aircraft was identical to the FB.11 and possessed a similar performance. FAA Sea Fury T.XXs were used to enable students to convert onto the type and to conduct weapons training.

RIGHT: Although the Gloster Meteor was designed to meet the RAF's requirement for a jet-powered fighter, the aircraft also proved to be successful as an advanced trainer. The prototype T.7 was manufactured from an existing F.4 airframe, the modification comprising a redesigned forward fuselage which incorporated a second cockpit. More than 650 aircraft were produced, and the trainer was used by both operational RAF squadrons and training units. Although the T.7 performed well, the aircraft suffered from poor directional stability thanks to the small tail surface. a larger-area tail was designed, resulting in the Meteor T.7 HTU (High tail Unit). The revised tail was employed on subsequent Meteor variants.

Gloster Meteor Trainer 19 March 1948

Supermarine Seagull ASR 14 July 1948

The Supermarine Type 381 Seagull (initially referred to as the Walrus Mk. II) emerged in 1940 as a replacement design for the Walrus and Sea Otter and an order for three prototypes was placed in 1943. Destined for the Air Sea Rescue role, the Seagull ASR. Mk. 1 first flew in July 1948. Powered by a 1,815hp Rolls-Royce Griffon engine (driving a contra-rotating propeller) the aircraft featured an unusual parasol wing which was attached to the fuselage by a single pylon. This enabled the entire wing's incidence to be varied, thanks to a pivoted front spar and an actuator unit attached to the rear. The second prototype performed carrier trials on Ark Royal during 1949 and although the design was successful, the aircraft's protracted development period rendered it obsolete, and no production order for the Fleet Air Arm was placed. The third prototype was not completed and all three aircraft were sold as scrap in 1952.

Hawker N7/46 (Sea Hawk) 3 September 1948

ABOVE: Although the Hawker Sea Hawk is regarded as an example of first-generation jet technology, Hawker's N.7/46 was, in effect, a derivative of the famous Sea Fury fighter, developed from studies which looked at modifying the Sea Fury/Fury airframe to accept a jet powerplant (the P.1035). As the design progressed virtually every part of the Fury's airframe was abandoned and eventually a simple, straight-winged fighter emerged, powered by a single Rolls-Royce Nene engine fed by wing-root-mounted intakes, emerging through a bifurcated exhaust which improved thrust and provided additional internal space for fuel. Flying for the first time on 2 September 1947, the P.1040 was developed for the FAA and proved to be an outstanding success. It entered FAA service in 1953 and remained in use until the late 1960s having operated in fighter, fighter-bomber, ground-attack and second-line roles (illustrated is a Fleet Requirements Unit example). The aircraft achieved considerable export success.

Gloster Meteor F Mk8 12 October 1948

LEFT: The successful Meteor was produced in several variants. The definitive fighter variant was the F.8 which became the RAF's main fighter aircraft 1950–55. Developed from the F.4, the first F.8 flew in 1948. The Meteor F.8 was developed for a variety of additional roles, not least PR and advanced training, and many other aircraft were assigned to trials work. Considerable export success was achieved with the F.8 and aircraft saw extensive service with many countries.

Avro Shackleton MR. Mk. 1 9 March 1949

ABOVE: Having developed the Lincoln from the wartime Lancaster, Avro produced the 696, a maritime reconnaissance and ASW version of the Lincoln, initially named the Lincoln ASR. Mk. 3. This design (later named Shackleton) became one of the RAF's most successful aircraft, equipping maritime squadrons from the early 1950s until the early 1970s. With the same general layout as the Lancaster (but with Lincoln wings, a larger fuselage and Griffon engines driving contra-rotating propellers), the Shackleton GR. Mk. 1 (later redesignated MR. Mk. 1) was a sturdy and reliable aircraft with excellent long-range capability (illustrated is a T.4 trainer derivative of the Mk. 1). The MR. Mk. 2 was a direct derivative of this design, featuring a larger nose section (with radar equipment moved to a ventral fuselage position) and upgraded equipment. One squadron of Mk. 2 Shackletons was later converted to AEW. Mk. 2 standard, acting as interim airborne early warning aircraft until a new, purpose-built AEW design could be brought into service. The protracted development (and subsequent abandonment) of the AEW Nimrod enabled these Shackletons to remain in service until 1991 when they were replaced by the E-3D Sentry.

RIGHT: Initially designed to be powered by the huge Rolls-Royce Eagle piston engine, development of the Wyvern strike fighter was dogged by engine problems and with a shortage of available engines, attention shifted to turboprop power in the shape of the Rolls-Royce Clyde and Armstrong Siddeley Python. Trials with a single Clyde-powered prototype were disappointing and the initial production batch of Wyvern TF.2 aircraft were powered by Pythons, a temperamental engine which required careful handling. Finally, the Python entered FAA service in 1953 as the TF.4 (later redesignated S.4), and this (together with a handful of modified TF.2s) embarked upon a short and troublesome career. The aircraft was used with some success in combat operations during the 1956 Suez Crisis, but by 1958, the Wyvern had largely been withdrawn from front-line service and the type was retired. The aircraft was ultimately a victim of its temperamental powerplant and the rapid development of jet aircraft design.

Westland Wyvern (A.S. Python engine)
22 March 1949

English Electric Canberra 13 May 1949

The English Electric Canberra was Britain's first jet bomber and can be regarded as one of the most significant post-war aircraft ever produced. Flying for the first time on Friday 13 May 1949, the Canberra entered RAF service in 1951, providing the force with a fast, high-altitude bomber which represented a quantum leap in capability when compared to the aged piston-engined Lincolns which were in use at the time. With vice-free handling, the Canberra's sprightly performance outclassed many contemporary fighter designs, providing the basis for a wide range of derivatives, suited to a variety of roles. In addition to the bomber types, the Canberra was developed as a high-altitude photo-reconnaissance aircraft, a target tug, radar trainer and trials aircraft, and with a production run of more than 900 aircraft, the type was highly successful in the export market, with sales being made to Argentina, Australia, Chile, Ecuador, Ethiopia, France, Germany, India, New Zealand, Peru, Rhodesia, South Africa, Sweden and Venezuela. Most significantly, the Canberra was adopted by the United States and produced under license as the B-57 with more than 400 aircraft being produced for the USAF in a variety of versions. Virtually all Canberras were finally withdrawn from operational use by the 1990s, the final RAF aircraft being retired in 2006 although a handful of aircraft remain active around the world performing specialised tasks, not least the remaining WB-57 aircraft (featuring redesigned high-lift wings and improved engines) which continue to fly with NASA.

Vickers Varsity   17 July 1949

ABOVE: Derived from the wartime Wellington bomber, the Type 668 Varsity was designed by Vickers as a navigational and multi-engine trainer for the RAF. Based on the Viking airliner (which retained the Wellington's wing layout, engines and undercarriage), the Varsity employed a redesigned tricycle undercarriage, improved engines (with new cowlings) and a larger tail area, together with a ventral fairing incorporating a small bomb bay for weapons training procedures. Flying for the first time in 1949 (prototype illustrated, top), the Varsity T.1 entered service in 1951 and remained in use in the navigation training role until the mid-1960s. It remained active in a variety of roles, and the last examples were retired in 1976. Although 160 were built, virtually all of the production aircraft were operated by the RAF, and only a handful were exported (to Jordan and Sweden), although a small number of aircraft were also assigned to test and research duties, primarily with the RAE. It was an RAE aircraft which made the last Varsity flight in July 1992 when the aircraft was delivered to the RAF Museum at Cosford.

RIGHT: The successful design of de Havilland's Vampire fighter led to a number of derivatives suited to various roles. Amongst these was the twin-seat DH.113 which retained the same wings and tail layout as the single seater, but incorporated a redesigned fuselage with twin seats fitted side-by-side under a new metal-framed canopy. Intended to serve as a prototype for a night fighter, the aircraft accommodated an AI.X radar unit in the nose and the aircraft's heavier all-up weight necessitated the instal-lation of an uprated Goblin 3 engine which gave the aircraft a marginally better performance than its single-seat predecessors. The first prototype of what became the Vampire NF.10 took place on 28 August 1949 with initial deliveries intended for the Egyptian Air Force. After a sales embargo was placed on Egypt the aircraft were diverted to the RAF. The NF.10 performed well, but it was regarded as an interim aircraft pending delivery of night fighter Venoms and Meteors. By the mid-1950s the aircraft had been withdrawn from operational use and allocated to navigational training duties, redesignated Vampire NF(T)10.

De Havilland Vampire Night Fighter 28 July 1949

De Havilland Venom 2 September 1949

Blackburn B.54 (YA.7) 20 September 1949

ABOVE LEFT: The de Havilland Venom was a direct development of the Vampire, designed to meet an RAF requirement for a more capable fighter-bomber. The origins of the aircraft lay in an aborted plan to develop the Vampire with a new thinner wing and powerful engine (the FB.8), and although the Venom retained a similarity to its predecessor (with a similar fuselage and tail), the aircraft had a completely re-designed wing and a more powerful Ghost engine. The prototype first flew on 2 September 1949 and entered service as the Venom FB.1 in 1952, some 375 aircraft being built. Armed with four 20mm cannon, the Venom could also carry two 1,000lb bombs or rocket projectiles. Although lightly armed and possessing a relatively modest performance, the Venom was a useful asset and participated in combat operations during the Malayan Emergency and in the Suez Crisis during which the aircraft flew attack missions against ground installations.

BELOW LEFT: Designed in response to a Naval requirement for a carrier-capable anti-submarine aircraft, Blackburn's B-54 (the YA.5) was one of two key programmes created to meet this requirement, the other being produced by Fairey. Although relatively conventional in design, the YA.5 featured an unorthodox inverted gull wing and was expected to be powered by a pair of Napier Naiad turboprop engines, connected to a contra-rotating propeller through a common gearbox. This engine was eventually abandoned and the YA.5 first flew on 20 September 1949 with a Rolls-Royce Griffon 58 piston engine, redesignated as the YA.7. Following further design specifications for radar equipment, the aircraft was refined still further and emerged as the YA.8 and ultimately the B-88 or YB.1 which first flew in 1950. Powered by an Armstrong Siddeley Double Mamba engine (as was Fairey's competing design, development and evaluation of the prototypes was a protracted process and the FAA eventually chose to adopt Fairey's design (which became the Gannet) and the Blackburn aircraft were all abandoned.

Fairey 17 Gannet 29 September 1949

ABOVE AND RIGHT: The Fairey Gannet emerged in response to an RN requirement for an ASW aircraft. A competing design was produced by Blackburn but ultimately it was Fairey's Type 17 (illustrated above) which was ordered. Powered by an Armstrong Siddeley Double Mamba, the Gannet made the first carrier landing by a turboprop-powered aircraft in 1950. The initial production version was the AS.1 of which 180 were built. These were followed by 35 T.2 trainers and the AS.4 with an uprated engine (the T.5 being a direct trainer derivative). Further developments included the AS.6 with improved radar and ASW equipment and the ECM.6, an ECM aircraft. The COD.4 was a carrier transport aircraft. Replaced by helicopters in the ASW role, the remaining COD Gannets were withdrawn in the mid-1970s.

Westland Wyvern Trainer 11 February 1950

Percival Provost 23 February 1950

Handley Page HPR.2 24 April 1950

ABOVE LEFT: Undoubtedly the least well-known derivative of the Westland Wyvern strike aircraft was the T.3 dual-control version of which only one example was built. Based on the standard TF.2 airframe, the T.3 incorporated a second cockpit, situated behind and above the existing standard position, the canopies being linked by a Perspex tunnel fairing. With duplicated controls and instruments, the aircraft was developed in anticipation of an order for conversion trainer Wyverns, but the FAA showed little interest in the proposal. Finished in a unique silver paint scheme (with yellow 'trainer bands' and prototype markings), the aircraft enjoyed only a brief test career. On 3 November 1950 the aircraft suffered an engine failure when the front propeller translation bearing seized, and this forced test pilot Sqn Ldr Don Colvin to glide-land the aircraft onto water meadows on the estuary of the River Axe near Seaton in Devon. Although the forced landing was successful, attempts to recover the aircraft from the mud resulted in extensive damage and when investigations revealed that the wing main spar had been twisted, the aircraft was scrapped.

BELOW LEFT: In response to an Air Ministry specification for an aircraft to replace the Prentice, Percival developed the P.56 Provost, a straight-winged, fixed-undercarriage tail-wheeled aircraft powered by a single Armstrong Siddeley Cheetah piston engine (later replaced by the Alvis Leonides). Designed as a basic trainer with a much superior performance as compared to Percival's sluggish Prentice, the prototype Provost first flew on 24 February 1950, entering service with the RAF in 1953. With good manoeuvrability, uncomplicated handling and a rugged construction, the Provost was popular with both instructors and students, and the type remained in active service until the mid-1960s, when the jet-powered derivative of the same aircraft (the Jet Provost) was introduced. Some examples of the type remained active in secondary roles, the final examples used for air traffic control training being withdrawn towards the end of the 1960s. Some 461 examples were built with exports being made to Burma, Iraq, Ireland, Malaysia, Rhodesia, Oman and Sudan. A few surviving examples remain airworthy under civilian ownership.

ABOVE: Although Percival Aircraft successfully produced the Provost trainer in response to the Air Ministry's Specification T.16/48, another serious contender for the order was the HPR.2 designed by Miles Aircraft (the company later becoming part of Handley Page). With similar side-by-side seating for student and instructor, the aircraft shared many similarities with the Provost but overall performance and handling proved to be inferior. Only two aircraft were completed, one powered by an Armstrong Siddeley Cheetah, the other by an Alvis Leonides piston, this aircraft being fitted with a re-designed fin and rudder. When the Provost was finally selected for production, further development of the HPR.2 was abandoned and the prototypes scrapped. With a top speed of 175mph (compared to the Provost's 200mph), the HPR.2 was a promising design, but undoubtedly inferior to the successful Provost.

Armstrong Whitworth Meteor Night Fighter 31 May 1950

ABOVE: Following the success of Gloster's Meteor fighter and trainer production, attention turned to night fighter variants, designed to replace the RAF's Mosquitos. Much of this work was delegated to Armstrong Whitworth, and virtually all of the subsequent night fighter models were manufactured at their Coventry factory. The initial version was the NF.Mk.11 (illustrated), based on the earlier T.7 airframe but with an extended nose housing intercept radar and an F.8-type fin, together with extended outer wings.

Machine guns were moved from the new nose out onto the wings and the prototype airframe (converted from a T7) first flew in May 1950 with deliveries to RAF squadrons continuing until 1955. The NF.12 was a similar design, taking advantage of a more capable APS-21 radar system, the NF.13 being a tropicalised version of the Mk.12, destined for operation in the Middle and Far East. The ultimate Meteor variant was the NF.14, which incorporated improved engines and radar and a much-needed bubble canopy

which improved the pilot's all-round vision. Largely replaced in RAF service by the Javelin, the Meteor night fighters were withdrawn through the late 1950s (the last being in service with No.60 Squadron in Singapore in 1961), but a small fleet of modified NF(T).14 aircraft remained active as high-speed navigation trainers until 1965 when they were replaced by the Dominie. Modest export sales for the NF.11 were achieved to many existing Meteor customers.

Blackburn B-88 (YB.1) 19 July 1950

LEFT: Blackburn's distinctive YB.1 (the B-88) held a great deal of promise as a potential anti-submarine warfare aircraft for the Fleet Air Arm's carrier squadrons. Developed from the YA.5 (B-54), the aircraft was manufactured at the company's Brough factory and first flew on 19 July 1950. Competing with similar designs from both Fairey and Shorts, the aircraft performed well and was marginally faster than the competing design being offered by Fairey. Despite being very similar in terms of general layout and even power plant (a pair of Mamba turboprops driving a contra-rotating propeller), the aircraft was abandoned after service trials, when the FAA selected Fairey's design (which became the Gannet). Although the YB.1 was designed to incorporate two crew members (as were the competing designs), a revised service requirement led to the Gannet being redesigned to accommodate three crew prior to adoption by the FAA.

Short SB.3 12 August 1950

ABOVE: Shorts responded to a requirement for a carrier-borne ASW aircraft by revising its existing SA.1 Sturgeon design. Although created as a target tug, the Sturgeon was adapted to undertake the ASW role, requiring a redesigned fuselage which supported a huge nose fairing in which the necessary radar (plus two operators) could be accommodated. The power plants were replaced by a pair of Mamba turboprops, but the combination of the huge bulbous nose and new turboprops led to handling difficulties. The

ASW contract eventually went to Fairey's Gannet and both the first prototype and the unflown second prototype were scrapped in 1951.

BELOW: Just as the Vampire was developed into the Venom, de Havilland redesigned the Vampire night fighter to incorporate the wings and engine improvements of the Venom, resulting in the Venom NF.2. It was manufactured in prototype form as part of a manufacturer-funded programme, there being little interest from the

Air Ministry. The aircraft was powered by a 4,950lb DH Ghost engine and the first production aircraft made its first flight in March 1953. Although the aircraft offered only modest improvements over the earlier Vampire night fighters, the type was purchased by the RAF and an improved version (the NF.3) entered service in 1955, some 129 aircraft being ordered. Four of these aircraft remained active as target tugs until 1971.

De Havilland Venom Night Fighter 22 August 1950

De Havilland Vampire Trainer 15 November 1950

ABOVE: Using company funds, de Havilland re-designed the single-seat Vampire fighter design to incorporate staggered side-by-side seating for two crew members and a housing for an intercept radar, creating the DH.113 nightfighter prototype which eventually entered service as the NF.10. The same fuselage configuration was developed still further to produce an advanced trainer. The pull-off radar housing was replaced by a more streamlined hinged nose, the staggered seating was repositioned to enable a student and instructor to sit side by side and the Goblin 3 engine was modified to incorporate a bleed system to deliver cabin pressurisation. Although early examples of this design (the Vampire T.11) did not incorporate ejection seats, they were introduced from the 144th aircraft onwards. Hugely successful as an advanced

trainer, the Vampire T.11 remained in service with the RAF until the early 1960s when the Folland Gnat was introduced. The type remained in use in many secondary roles for many years, the final examples (used for air traffic control training) being retained into the early 1970s. Not surprisingly, many export customers also purchased the Vampire trainer and Switzerland retained the aircraft in service until 1999.

BELOW: The Royal Navy expressed an interest in de Havilland's Venom NF.2 as a potential replacement for the FAA's Sea Hornet. Suitability trials (including touch-and-go landings) led to the production of three prototypes of what became the Sea Venom NF.20. Suitably modified with strengthened undercarriage, folding wings and a tail hook, the Mk.20 entered service in

1954. The FAW.21 followed (some 167 being produced) featuring an improved canopy, underwater ejection modifications, improved radar and engines and boosted controls. The ultimate Sea Venom variant was the FAW.22 (39 produced), featuring a 5,150lb Ghost engine, improved AI.22 radar and an ability to carry air-to-air missiles – the first such FAA aircraft. Used extensively through the late 1950s and into the 1960s, the Sea Venom was a successful fighter-bomber used both by front-line units (including participation in the Suez Crisis) and second line units with which the aircraft remained active until the early 1970s. France also adopted the Sea Venom (named 'Aquilon') and continued operating the type until 1960.

De Havilland Sea Venom 19 April 1951

Vickers Valiant 18 May 1951

ABOVE: Built as part of the famous trio of V-Class strategic bombers for the RAF, the Type 660 was proposed by Vickers as an interim design which could be brought into service more reliably and swiftly than the Vulcan and Victor aircraft which were being developed by Avro and Handley Page. The 660 (later named Valiant) was a simplified swept-wing design which lacked the performance of the more advanced Vulcan and Victor, but was sufficiently capable to warrant service production. The type was ordered for the RAF following the Valiant's first flight on 18 May 1951. Fitted with four 10,000lb Avon engines, the Valiant was able to carry a single Blue Danube atomic bomb – the RAF's first generation nuclear weapon. Although proven to be a reliable and capable bomber (also used in the reconnaissance and aerial tanker roles), the Valiant's service life was cut short prematurely following the switch to low-level *operations during the 1960s. Metal alloys chosen for the aircraft's construction had led to unforeseen fatigue problems and low-level operations rapidly contributed to severe damage to the Valiant's wing spar structure. The type was immediately withdrawn in January 1965. Only one complete example of the Valiant remains, this being in the RAF Museum at Cosford.*

Fairey Firefly AS.7 22 May 1951

RIGHT: The Fairey Firefly fighter became the basis for a range of redesigned variants, each suited to a specific role. The initial production model provided the basis for fighter, reconnaissance and ASW versions, whilst later, more powerful derivatives took on similar roles plus many more, these aircraft taking advantage of improvements in the Griffon engine's power availability as its development continued. The AS.7 ended the Firefly's production, this variant being tailored to the AS role with a redesigned airframe, a 'beard' radiator (supplying a Griffon 59 engine) and accommodation for three crew members. Few AS.7s saw operational service, the majority being destined for ASW training duties, re-designated as the T.7, and some of these aircraft were later converted for unmanned target drone use, becoming the victims of Firestreak AAMs and Sea Slug missiles fired from the FAA's fighters and surface ships.

Hawker P1067 Hunter 20 July 1951

One of the most successful and versatile fighter aircraft ever produced, the Hunter's origins can be traced back to Hawker's World War II-era Sea Fury piston-engined fighter-bomber. Hawker conducted studies into developing the Fury into a jet-powered fighter and this eventually led to the creation of the Sea Hawk which served with the FAA for many years. Hawker explored the concept of creating a faster and more manoeuvrable swept-wing version of the Sea Hawk (the P.1052), but this did not generate significant interest for the Air Ministry. However, a later requirement for a jet-powered day fighter enabled Hawker to create the P.1067 which first flew on 20 July 1951 and became the basis for a production aircraft – the Hunter F.1. Utilising earlier swept-wing design knowledge, the Hunter took advantage of the then new 7,600lb thrust Rolls-Royce Avon axial-flow turbojet and a modified version of the aircraft set a new world speed record of 727.63mph in 1953. Almost 2,000 Hunters were eventually built in a range of variants, equipping RAF fighter, reconnaissance and ground-attack squadrons, and export sales were extremely successful with aircraft being sold to (or licence-built by) Belgium, Chile, Denmark, Jordan, the Netherlands, Sweden (illustrated below), Switzerland (illustrated left) and many other countries.

De Havilland DH 110 26 September 1951

ABOVE: De Havilland's DH.110 was designed in response to an emerging requirement for a gun- or missile-armed all-weather fighter which would be required by both the RAF and FAA. RAF interest eventually shifted in favour of the Gloster Javelin but naval interest in the design continued and the type was developed for FAA service as a successor to the Sea Venom. The prototype first flew on 26 September 1951 and although designed with manoeuvrability and speed in mind (powered by two Avon turbojets), the aircraft earned the distinction of being the last British combat aircraft to use wood as part of its construction, with wooden reinforcements installed in the gun mountings. Although the aircraft was ultimately developed into the highly successful Sea Vixen fighter, the DH.110 prototype's short test career came to a tragic end in 1952 when it broke up following a supersonic demonstration at the SBAC Farnborough show, the accident being caused by wrongly designed main spar construction.

ABOVE RIGHT: The Gloster Javelin was designed in response to an Air Ministry requirement for an all-weather day and night fighter – something that the Royal Navy was also seeking – and this led to the development of a competing design from de Havilland. The RAF eventually concluded that the Javelin appeared to be a more promising design and the DH.110 was abandoned, although the Navy pursued that project which ultimately produced the Sea Vixen. Flying for the first time on 26 November 1951, the first 14 Javelin FAW.1s were delivered in 1956. The aircraft was developed into more powerful versions, the ultimate being the FAW.9 (illustrated) which was powered by a pair of reheated 12,300lb Sapphire engines. Some 14 squadrons were equipped with the Javelin in the early 1960s, but the aircraft's modest performance and demanding handling character-istics ensured that it was rapidly replaced by Hunters and Lightnings, the last operational example being withdrawn in 1968. The final flying Javelin was a Mk.9 which remained in use with the A&AEE at Boscombe Down until 1975.

RIGHT: Developed from Supermarine's successful straight-winged Attacker fighter, the Swift was designed for the RAF as a potential replacement for the Meteor and, to some extent, as insurance against the possible failure of the emerging Hunter being produced by Hawker. The Swift emerged from a complex develop-mental history, embracing three basic designs that ultimately resulted in the Swift F.1 which entered service in 1954. With a pair of Aden cannon, it was the RAF's first swept-wing fighter. Unfortunately, the Swift's early operational history was marred by accidents and long periods of enforced grounding as a result of various handling problems which plagued the aircraft. Ultimately, it was regarded as a failure as a useful fighter aircraft and it was quickly replaced by the Hunter as soon as that aircraft became available. However, the Swift was modified to undertake the low-level reconnaissance role and as the FR.5, the aircraft was a considerable success, being employed largely in Germany and remaining in use until replaced by the Hunter in 1961.

Gloster GA5 Javelin 26 November 1951

Supermarine Swift 25 August 1952

Avro 698 Vulcan 30 August 1952

Undoubtedly one of the most famous of all RAF aircraft, the Avro 698 Vulcan was created in response to the Air Ministry's urgent requirement for a long-range jet bomber capable of delivering the then-new atomic bomb. Based on World War II German research, Avro produced a variety of preliminary designs all of which employed a futuristic 'flying wing' layout. However by the time the 698 (illustrated left) reached prototype stage (flying for the first time on 30 August 1952), it had become a delta-shaped aircraft with a conventional forward fuselage (which was originally designed to be jettisoned in an emergency). Entering service as the Vulcan B.1 late in 1956, the aircraft was swiftly developed to take advantage of improvements in engine thrust and the Vulcan B.2 entered service in 1960. Armed with free-fall nuclear bombs (and subsequently a rocket-powered stand-off bomb), the aircraft formed the basis of Britain's independent nuclear deterrent through the 1960s. After continuing in service as a free-fall bomber and maritime radar reconnaissance aircraft until the 1980s (and performing the longest bomber flight in British military history during the 1982 Falklands conflict), the last Vulcans (employed as tankers) were retired in 1984. Just one civilian-owned Vulcan remains airworthy, this being XH558, the first B.2 to enter RAF service and the last to be withdrawn.

Handley Page Victor 25 December 1952

ABOVE AND LEFT: *Handley Page's HP.80 Victor was the third of the RAF's three V-Bombers to enter into operational service. Flying for the first time on 24 December 1952, the Victor B.1 followed the Valiant and Vulcan into service, operating as a free-fall nuclear bomber. The later B.2 (with Rolls-Royce Conway engines) was employed initially in the same role although when operations switched to low level, the Victor's relatively flexible wings made the aircraft less than ideal for the role, and loading stand-off missiles under the aircraft's low-slung fuselage was difficult. The Victors were re-assigned as tankers (following the Valiant's premature retirement) and became a vital part of modern operations, remaining in use until replaced by the VC-10 in October 1983. A small number of Victors were also assigned to the strategic reconnaissance role until replaced by Vulcans. The Victor was undoubtedly the most advanced of the V-Bomber designs, with the greatest speed (one aircraft having exceeded the speed of sound in a dive during 1956), altitude and bomb-carrying capacity, but ultimately the Vulcan proved to be the most versatile of the trio. Illustrated (above) is a B.1 engaged in SLAR (Sideways Looking Airborne Radar) trials.*

Short Seamew 28 August 1953

ABOVE: The curiously shaped SB.6 Seamew enjoyed only a very brief operational history. The aircraft was intended as a relatively simple, lightweight anti-submarine warfare aircraft designed to replace the Avenger in FAA service, primarily for use by the Royal Naval Volunteer Reserve. Three prototypes were produced, the first making its maiden flight on 23 August 1953. Although the RAF was also expected to purchase the aircraft, it eventually lost interest in the programme and it was the Royal Navy which finally ordered a batch of aircraft for the RNVR. Unfortunately, the RNVR was disestablished in 1957 at which stage only four aircraft had actually been delivered. Ultimately, just seven aircraft reached the FAA and these were quickly placed in storage at Lossiemouth before being scrapped. The Seamew featured some innovative design, not least the Mamba turboprop engine which minimised the vibration that disturbed radar screens. Furthermore, the tail-wheel undercarriage enabled the Seamew's radar to achieve a good, uncluttered forward view. A great deal of design work was devoted to the wing structure, but even by the time the aircraft reached the production stage it was accepted that the Seamew's performance was relatively disappointing and the aircraft handled very poorly. The Seamew's promising career was ultimately ended by the infamous 1957 Defence Review which effectively rendered the aircraft redundant.

Vickers Valiant B.2 4 September 1953

RIGHT: The Valiant's career was cut short when it began to experience metal fatigue problems, compounded by the shift to low-level operations in the 1960s. Some consideration was given to modifications, but the cost was outweighed by the amount of time for which the Valiant would still be required. Ironically, Vickers had already designed a variant which was specifically geared to low-level operations. The Valiant B.2 was designed as a low-level pathfinder bomber, strengthened for the stresses of low flying. Although similar in external appearance to the B.1, the B.2 featured a longer fuselage and, due to the strengthened wing structure, the undercarriage was repositioned in external fairings on the wing trailing edge. The Air Ministry ordered 17 aircraft, but after the first prototype was completed, the order was cancelled after having been judged unnecessary and expensive. With the benefit of hindsight, it is clear that the Valiant B.2 would have been perfectly suited to the low-level role.

Auster AOP.9 19 March 1954

Hunting Percival Jet Provost
26 June 1954

TOP: Manufactured as a direct replacement for the Auster AOP.6, the AOP.9 featured a re-designed wing and more powerful engine. The AOP.9 had a pilot and passenger plus an observer. The aircraft could also be converted into a light transport. Deliveries to the RAF began in 1956 with further aircraft going to the AAC. Remaining in use until 1966, the AOP.9 was the Army's last fixed-wing air observation aircraft, the light transport role being taken over by Beavers.

ABOVE: Much loved by thousands of RAF pilots, the Jet Provost was the RAF's basic jet trainer through the 1960s and 1970s. Created as an aircraft to replace the Percival Provost, the Jet Provost was a direct jet-powered derivative which was externally similar to its piston-engined counterpart. Entering service in 1957 the faithful Jet Provost continued on until the 1990s when it was replaced by the Tucano. Export sales were good, particularly for the armed version of the Jet Provost T.5 – the Strikemaster.

English Electric Canberra B.8 23 July 1954

ABOVE: The Canberra B.8 became the RAF's primary interdictor aircraft through the 1960s and early 1970s, with some aircraft being assigned to the delivery of Red Beard free-fall tactical nuclear bombs (for which a number of aircraft were maintained on 'Battle Flight' alert status). Essentially a development of the B.6, the Canberra B(I)8 featured a re-designed forward fuselage, and a smaller fighter-type cockpit placed offset to port to give the pilot good all-round visibility. The navigator was positioned alongside the pilot but lower inside the fuselage under an escape hatch (both crew having ejection seats). As a night/all-weather intruder, the B(I)8 was equipped with a Boulton Paul-designed gun pack which fitted into the bomb bay, emerging under the fuselage in a fairing. The Canberra was well suited to the low-level role and crews also regularly practised LABS (Low Altitude Bombing System) deliveries for their nuclear role, requiring the aircraft to be pulled into a vertical climb before rolling off the top of the ensuing loop. The Canberra B(I)8 remained in service until 1972 when it was replaced by the Phantom.

Folland Midge 11 August 1954

De Havilland Sea Vixen 20 June 1955

LEFT: Better known as the designer of the Canberra, W.E.W. 'Teddy' Petter left English Electric to pursue his interest in the concept of lightweight jet-fighter design. Concerned with the growing complexity and expense of fighter designs such as the Lightning, he became convinced there was potential for creating a smaller, less complicated and less expensive fighter which took advantage of new lightweight turbojet designs. Having re-located to Folland, Petter created the Fo-141 Gnat, a simple swept-wing design powered by a 3,800lb Bristol BE-22 Saturn turbojet. However, the Saturn was subsequently cancelled and Petter's proof-of-concept demonstrator emerged with a 1,640lb Viper engine. Redesignated as the Fo-139 Midge, the aircraft was evaluated by pilots from Canada, India, Jordan, New Zealand and the USAF before being destroyed under evaluation by a Swiss pilot in September 1955. The aircraft had undoubtedly been a success, however, and Folland used company funds to create an improved version of the design which became the definitive Gnat lightweight fighter/trainer.

BELOW LEFT: Following the withdrawal of RAF interest in the DH.110 (the Javelin being selected as the RAF's next all-weather fighter), the RN remained keen to see it developed into a production fighter and the first Sea Vixen FAW.20 (later redesignated as the FAW.1) emerged in 1957 (illustrated), the first of over 100 aircraft which began to enter service with the FAA in 1959. Development culminated in the FAW.2 (some of these being converted from existing Mk. 1 airframes) which was capable of carrying Red Top and Bullpup missiles as well as SNEB rocket launchers. Externally similar to the Mk. 1, the Sea Vixen Mk. 2 incorporated lengthened tail boom fairings which extended beyond the leading edge of the aircraft's wing, providing space for additional fuel. With the arrival of the Phantom, the Sea Vixen was withdrawn in 1972 although some were subsequently converted into unmanned target drones (the D.3). A plan to convert a significant number to D.3 standard was abandoned due to cost considerations but also because the Vixen proved to be less than ideal for the role.

BELOW: Although the single-seat fighter and ground-attack derivatives of the Hunter were built in large quantities, a significant number of Hunters were completed as twin-seat conversion trainers, designated as the T.7 (RAF) and T.8 (FAA). Although logic would dictate that this aircraft ought to have been based on the F.6, the twin-seater design was actually based on the F.4. With a redesigned forward fuselage, the dual-control Hunter retained the same performance and handling as the F.4. The design featured a twin-bubble canopy layout, although this was later abandoned – but in all other respects the development of the T.7 was remarkably straightforward. Initially assigned to the RAF's weapons training unit (229 OCU) the Hunter T.7 went on to serve with virtually all of the RAF's Hunter units. By the early 1970s most of the remaining twin-seat Hunters were assigned to the Navy's Fleet Requirements and Air Direction Unit, although others still remained in service with the RAF, equipped with Buccaneer instrumentation for conversion training.

Hawker P1101 Hunter Trainer 8 July 1955

Folland Gnat Fighter 18 July 1955

LEFT: Although generally regarded as a successful advanced trainer aircraft, Folland's Gnat was originally designed as a lightweight fighter. Although the proof-of-concept prototype (the Midge) was lost during an evaluation flight, confidence in the design encouraged Folland to proceed with the construction of an improved version of this aircraft, incorporating aerodynamic refinements with larger air intakes and provision for a pair of 30mm cannon. As a relatively inexpensive lightweight aircraft, the Gnat was purchased by both Finland and India, where it was manufactured under licence and remained in use in operational and second-line roles until the 1990s. Many Gnats (named 'Ajeet' for Indian service) flew combat missions during conflicts in both Pakistan and India. The RAF also evaluated the aircraft but interest in the Gnat was abandoned when the more capable Hawker Hunter became available. Although the lightweight fighter concept had many advantages, the Gnat's cramped layout ensured that maintenance of the aircraft was always difficult and cockpit space was always at a minimum. As an inexpensive and simple aircraft however, the diminutive Gnat proved to be a surprisingly agile and capable fighter.

BELOW: Having successfully produced the Mk. 1 and Mk. 2 variants of the Shackleton for RAF service, Avro proceeded to design a more advanced version of the aircraft which resulted in the Shackleton MR.3. Although essentially similar to earlier versions, the Mk. 3 employed a tricycle undercarriage layout (eliminating the last vestiges of similarity with its Lancaster heritage) and featured improved wing design (with wingtip-mounted fuel tanks), an enlarged nose section, re-designed flight deck windows (providing better visibility), and much-improved crew accommodation. Significantly heavier (by some 30,000lb) than the Mk. 2, the new Mk. 3 suffered from a degraded take-off performance and this prompted Avro to produce the Shackleton Mk. 3 Phase 3 aircraft, which incorporated Viper turbojets in the outer engine nacelles to provide useful additional thrust. Although the aircraft performed well and was popular with the RAF's crews, the heavier Mk. 3 fell victim to higher fatigue stresses and, with some irony, tended to wear out ahead of the older Mk. 2 aircraft. Consequently, although the MR.2 soldiered on in RAF service for many years, the MR.3 was withdrawn from use by 1971. After evaluating the Shackleton, South Africa opted to purchase eight of the Mk. 3 variant and these were operated with great success by the SAAF until 1984. One aircraft from this fleet is preserved in flying condition.

Avro Shackleton MR.3 2 September 1955

Supermarine Type 544 Scimitar 19 January 1956

ABOVE: The Scimitar was the result of a naval requirement for a single-seat jet fighter. The prototype Scimitar first flew in January 1956 (the first 'true' Scimitar flying a year later) and 100 aircraft were ordered (76 were built), entering service in 1957. The Scimitar enjoyed a relatively short service life. The fighter role was ultimately undertaken by the Sea Vixen and after the introduction of the Buccaneer in the strike role, the Scimitar was relegated to use as a carrier-borne tanker.

BELOW LEFT: The English Electric P.1B Lightning earned the distinction of being the RAF's very last all-British fighter aircraft and was also the only British operational fighter to have been capable of sustained supersonic flight. Operations began in 1960 and the Lightning became a fundamental part of the RAF's air defence structure, further orders being made for more powerful and agile versions in the form of the F.2 (and F.2A), F.3 and F.6. The Lightning proved to be a capable and useful interceptor which remained in service with the RAF until the late 1980s.

English Electric P.1B Lightning 4 April 1957

Blackburn NA.39 Buccaneer 30 April 1958

ABOVE: Blackburn's B-103 was created in response to an Admiralty requirement for a high-speed strike fighter capable of countering the emerging 'Sverdlov' class of Soviet cruisers. Essentially, the RN required a carrier-launched aircraft which could deliver a single atomic bomb at low level. The aircraft was developed into a production-standard aircraft which entered service in 1962 as the Buccaneer S.1. This was later augmented (and eventually replaced) by the more powerful S.2 (powered by a pair of Spey turbofans). Despite the Buccaneer S.1's modest performance, the S.2 was a very capable aircraft and, following cancellation of the TSR.2 programme, the RAF also ordered the Buccaneer (46 examples) and took on many of the FAA's aircraft when the last carrier was withdrawn. Serving with distinction until 1984, the Buccaneer took part in operations around the world, including bombing missions during the infamous Torrey Canyon incident, and a significant laser designation role during the Gulf War. Exports were confined to South Africa, where the aircraft remained active until 1991.

RIGHT: The Canberra's excellent altitude and speed ability made the aircraft an ideal reconnaissance platform and even before a dedicated reconnaissance version was designed, one RAF squadron employed a handful of Canberra bombers on reconnaissance duties. The PR.3 was the first purpose-built variant designed for the role and this was followed by the PR.7. Both were conversions of the standard Canberra airframe, modified to accommodate cameras. However, to create a more capable high-altitude reconnaissance platform for the RAF, English Electric completely redesigned the aircraft and produced the Canberra PR.9. Using the standard Canberra fuselage, the wings were increased in length and chord and new, more powerful Avon 206 engines were installed in redesigned cowlings. The 'greenhouse' canopy was replaced by a B.8-style offset canopy, and the nose section was also hinged to enable the navigator to access his relocated position in the nose section ahead of the pilot. Production of the PR.9 was subcontracted to Shorts and some 23 aircraft were built, the first entering service in January 1960. The PR.9's unique capabilities ensured that the RAF continued to operate the aircraft for decades; the final examples of the type were finally retired in July 2006. Exports were confined to three aircraft which were transferred to Chile after the Falklands conflict.

English Electric Canberra PR.9
26 July 1958

Fairey Gannet AEW.3   29 August 1958

English Electric Lightning Trainer

6 May 1959

TOP: The AEW Gannet was intended to to carry the Skyraider's AN-APS-20F radar in an external fairing under the fuselage. However, accommodating the radar and operating crew required significant changes to the airframe. The completed aircraft retained much of the Gannet's appearance but in many respects was a new aircraft. Some 44 were built, and it remained in FAA service until the 1970s when the AEW role was assumed by the Shackleton AEW.3 fitted with radars from from retired Gannets.

ABOVE: The Lightning was produced in twin-seat form as a dual-control trainer, necessary for pilot conversion. The basic design was revised to incorporate seating for an instructor and student. The first trainers were T.4s; the later T.5s were derivatives of the F.3. Further examples were also manufactured for export to Saudi Arabia (illustrated) and Kuwait, these being based on the later F.6s. A handful of T.5s remain active in airworthy condition under civilian ownership.

Folland Gnat Trainer 31 August 1959

ABOVE: Although initial RAF interest in the Folland Gnat fighter was short-lived, the Air Ministry later issued a specification for a twin-seat advanced trainer which could take students through the transition from basic flying training on the Vampire (and later the Jet Provost) through to operational training on front-line types. Folland proposed the Fo.144 and it was accepted for production as the Gnat T.1. Used almost exclusively for advanced training at RAF Valley, the Gnat had sufficiently demanding handling skills to give students good training experience. The only downside was that the cockpit was too small for larger students and so a batch of Hunters was assigned to Valley. The Gnat was adopted by the Red Arrows (illustrated), and remained in use with this unit after all other RAF Gnats had been retired, until replaced by Hawks during 1979. Although its version was slightly different in terms of design and equipment, India also operated twin-seat Gnat trainers built by HAL and known as the Ajeet Trainer in Indian service.

Hawker Siddeley P.1127 Kestrel 7 March 1964

ABOVE: The concept of creating a vertical take off and landing (VTOL) aircraft was first examined by Hawker after Bristol Aero-Engine's engineers approached the company with a radical new concept of vectoring thrust from a single engine, in 1957. Drawing on French research, Bristol created a completely new engine based on existing Orpheus and Olympus models, but with the engine's thrust directed through four swivelling nozzles. This new power plant (the Pegasus) formed the basis of a VTOL design which would meet a NATO requirement for a lightweight tactical support fighter. Official support was not forthcoming, however, and Hawker managed the development with significant funding from America, eventually producing two prototypes with a further two being funded by the Ministry of Supply. These aircraft (as the P.1127) proved the VTOL concept (flying for the first time on 7 July 1961 following hovering trials) and nine improved versions of the P.1127 were ordered to act as evaluation aircraft. These machines (as the Kestrel FGA.1) entered service with a tripartite evaluation unit

during 1965. The unit included personnel from the RAF, USAF and Luftwaffe with all three services interested in the aircraft. The trials were successful and although Germany later abandoned interest in the Kestrel, both the UK and US eventually ordered the refined operational-standard version of the aircraft – the famous Harrier.

RIGHT: The TSR.2 was one of British industry's finest technical triumphs, but the whole programme was later betrayed by political ineptitude. The Tactical Strike and Reconnaissance tasking was designed to create a supersonic replacement for the versatile Canberra bomber, but there was also an element of the strategic bomber. Nine aircraft were ordered at first: this was increased to 20, and then an initial production batch of 30 was added. The prototype (XR219 – the only aircraft ever to fly) was outwardly showing great promise during its early tests, and industrial centres all over the country were gearing-up to participate in the programme …. when suddenly, it was all

over. On 6 April 1965 it was announced that the whole TSR.2 programme had been cancelled.

BAC TSR.2 27 September 1964

Hawker Siddeley Dominie 30 December 1964

ABOVE: The Dominie replaced the RAF's lumbering Varsity and converted Meteor night fighters in the navigational training role from 1965. An off-the-shelf purchase of an existing business jet (the HS125), it was fitted with navigational equipment and became a flying classroom. Ideally suited to the role, the Dominie remains in service and nine aircraft now provide the RAF with a fast (top speed almost 500mph) and rugged training platform in which Weapons Systems Operators, Air Loadmasters and Air Engineers can practice their skills. Part of the Dominie fleet was upgraded in 1996 with new systems and equipment. The remainder was withdrawn, many being relegated to use as ground instructional airframes. Further examples of the HS125 jet were also purchased by the RAF for communications and light transport duties, two being assigned to The Queen's Flight at Northolt. The successful design remains in production for the civilian market in a much-modified form, produced by Hawker Raytheon, and more than 1,000 examples have been built.

Hawker Siddeley Harrier GR Mk1 31 August 1966

BELOW LEFT: Following successful trials of the Hawker Kestrel FGA.1, the RAF ordered a batch of 60 production aircraft. These were based on the design of the Kestrel but featured many refinements with new intakes, revised wing shape and other modifications. The first Harrier GR.1 made its maiden flight on 28 December 1967 and entered service in 1969 with No. 1 Squadron at Wittering as the world's first operational VTOL fixed-wing aircraft. Although possessing some demanding handling character-istics (which led to many accidents) the Harrier proved to be a very effective warplane. Surprisingly, America's interest in the project began to drift and it was the USMC which eventually opted to adopt the Harrier, and 113 AV-8A aircraft were manufactured (in the UK and US), these being based on the GR.1 airframe but with an uprated engine. Exports of the AV-8A were later made to Spain, which eventually sold its aircraft to Thailand. The early Harrier GR.1 was later modified to GR.3 standard (and new-build aircraft ordered) with upgraded equipment, not least a Laser Rangefinder and Marked Target Seeker in the nose; this became the ultimate development of the early Harrier airframe. Successfully operated by the RAF, the Harrier GR.3 played a significant part in the 1982 Falklands conflict.

BELOW RIGHT: Developed as a successor to the Shackleton, the Nimrod was one of a variety of designs proposed by British manufacturers to meet an RAF requirement for a new ASW aircraft also capable of performing maritime reconnaissance and SAR duties. The successful proposal was made by Hawker Siddeley, its design based on the Comet. The wings and fuselage remained virtually unchanged, but a large weapons bay was created (the largest ever fitted to a British aircraft) resulting in a bulged lower fuselage which extended beyond the original Comet's nose, creating a 'double bubble' fuselage with a revised nose profile housing a radar unit. The Avon engines were replaced by more powerful and economical Spey turbofans (requiring larger intakes and fairings) and the fin's area was extended, a large forward fillet being attached. The Nimrod MR.1 entered RAF service in October 1969 at St. Mawgan. Three Nimrods were assigned to the Elint (Electronic Intelligence) role, these being identified by the lack of MAD (Magnetic Anomaly Detector) boom which is attached to the tails of all other Nimrods. From 1975 the Nimrod fleet was upgraded to MR.2 standard with new radar and sensor equipment. Additionally, the aircraft was given an aerial refuelling capability, largely as a result of the Falklands conflict in which the Nimrod participated. Hugely successful and versatile, the Nimrod remained in service pending the delivery of the new-generation Nimrod MRA.4.

BAC 145 Jet Provost T.5   28 February 1967

ABOVE: The RAF's need for a pressurised basic trainer saw Hunting-Percival embark on a development programme using two T.4s, which were fitted with new nose sections featuring a larger pressurised cockpit and a one-piece sliding canopy. The same side-by-side seating was retained and in all other respects the aircraft remained virtually identical to the T.4 even retaining the same Viper engine. After evaluation at Boscombe Down, 110 Jet Provost T.5s were ordered, and the type went on to serve with the RAF's flying training units until 1991 when replaced by the Tucano. The last T.5s to leave RAF service were the T.5Bs assigned to high-speed navigation training. These aircraft remained in service until 1993.

Hawker Siddeley Nimrod MR.1

23 May 1967

BELOW: Building on the export sales success of the Jet Provost, BAC developed the pressurised Jet Provost Mk. 5 into a more capable trainer and light-attack aircraft. It formed the basis for the BAC 167 Strikemaster. Although still very much a Jet Provost, it incorporated many improvements such as more capable ejection seats, a more powerful 3,410lb-thrust engine, armour plating and strengthened wings which could be fitted with hard points for the carriage of bombs or rockets. The aircraft could also be fitted with a pair of machine guns. Saudi Arabia took delivery of the first examples (47 produced). South Yemen (illustrated) and the SAAF followed. Kuwait also purchased the Strikemaster and after a successful 15-year career the aircraft were returned to the manufacturer and refurbished prior to being sold to Botswana. Further sales were made to Ecuador, Kenya and New Zealand where the aircraft remained in service with the RNZAF for some twenty years.

RIGHT: The Jaguar was initially proposed as a replacement for the F-100, Mystere IV, F-84F and T-33A which were in service with the Armée de l'Air. Breguet's Br212 was selected to be produced in five versions, these being single-seaters for ground attack and nuclear strike and twin-seaters for tactical and advanced training. With Britain seeking an aircraft to fulfil its own training and support roles, an agreement between the two countries was achieved, resulting in SEPECAT - the Société Européenne de Production de l'Avion ECAT (École et Appui Tactique). Eight prototypes were produced, three in Britain and five in France. Eventually a batch of 40 dual-control Jaguar Es were ordered for the French Air Force and these were assigned to continuation and operational conversion training, remaining in use until the type's withdrawal from service in 1995. Similar to British twin-seaters, the Jaguar E did not have the single-seater's retractable refuelling probe, but bolt-on fixed probes were subsequently fitted to the AdlA fleet. Unlike their British counterparts, the aircraft were never fitted with uprated engines.

BELOW RIGHT: Taking delivery of the first production Jaguar in 1973, the French Air Force operated a fleet of 160 Jaguar A (attaque) aircraft until the type was retired in 1995. The Jaguar A was a more austere aircraft than much of the RAF aircraft's equipment. Underpowered, the French Jaguars were never fitted with upgraded engines, this doubtless being due to the absorption of Breguet into Dassault, which did not want to see the Jaguar competing with its own design (the Mirage F1) on the export market. Assigned to ground-attack and offensive support duties, Jaguar A was also assigned to low-level strike duties equipped with a 25kT AN52 nuclear store. Additionally, some Jaguar As were also operated in the SEAD (Suppression of Enemy Defences) role, armed with Martel anti-radar missiles. Because the Jaguar A had a built-in refuelling probe, it was often assigned to overseas commitments in locations such as Dakar, Chad and of course the Middle East during Operation Desert Storm. Although regarded as an underpowered and disappointing design (at least in French service) the Jaguar was a rugged and versatile aircraft, appreciated and admired by those who flew it.

BAC 167 Strikemaster 26 October 1967

SEPECAT Jaguar two seat (France) 8 September 1968

SEPECAT Jaguar single seat (France) 29 March 1969

Hawker Siddeley Harrier Trainer 24 April 1969

ABOVE: Although the Harrier GR.1 entered service in 1969, the RAF's initial training was complicated by the lack of a twin-seat dual-control variant. It was not until July 1970 that the first Harrier T.2 arrived at Wittering. A development of the single-seat GR.1, in the T.2 (illustrated) the instructor's cockpit was positioned behind and above the student's cockpit, resulting in a much longer forward fuselage. To counter the larger forward mass, the rear of the Harrier was also increased with a taller fin and longer tail fairing, which was later redesigned. Ten were produced and these were later upgraded to T.2A and a further four aircraft were built. When the single-seat

Harriers were modified to GR.3 standard the T.2s were converted to their equivalent T.4. They remained in use until both the GR.3 and T.4 were replaced by the second-generation Harrier GR.5–9 series of aircraft from 1987.

BELOW: Developed from the successful Beagle Pup, the Bulldog was designed for the military market as a twin-seat basic trainer, with space to accommodate a third crew member if necessary. First purchased by Sweden, some 130 aircraft were ordered in 1972 as replacements for the Chipmunk, remaining in service until 2000-2001.

ABOVE RIGHT: British interest in the Jaguar initially centred on the need for an advanced trainer, but its emerging capabilities encouraged the RAF to regard it as a potential offensive support aircraft. Thus the Jaguar was adopted (165 ordered) as a replacement for the Phantom, enabling that aircraft to be reassigned to air defence duties. The first Jaguars entered RAF service in 1974 at Lossiemouth, with ground-attack squadrons formed at Coltishall. The versatile Jaguar also became a vital part of the RAF Germany structure, both as a tactical support aircraft and also as a tactical strike aircraft armed with a single WE.177 nuclear bomb. Already better equipped than their French counterparts, the RAF Jaguars were upgraded from GR.1 to GRA.1A and eventually GR.4 standard with a new cockpit and equipment and uprated engines. Having served in both Gulf Wars, the Jaguar became a valuable part of the RAF's offensive capability. The remaining Jaguars were withdrawn from RAF service in 2007 to make way for the multi-role Typhoon aircraft, with the Tornado fleet taking on the bulk of the Jaguar's air-to-ground role.

RIGHT: In addition to an order for single-seat Jaguars the RAF also received 35 T.2 twin-seat aircraft. Similar to their single-seat counterparts, the Jaguar T.2 featured a lengthened fuselage incorporating a second cockpit for an instructor, but in all other respects the airframe remained unchanged. The twin-seaters were also the subject of later upgrades both to T.2A, T.2B (with TIALD capability) and eventually T.4 standard. RAF operations for all Jaguars ended in April 2007 but a pair of twin-seaters remained in use with QinetiQ at Boscombe Down until December of the same year.

Beagle Bulldog 19 May 1969

SEPECAT Jaguar single seat (UK) 12 October 1969

SEPECAT Jaguar two seat (UK) 30 August 1971

Panavia Tornado IDS (Germany) 17 August 1974

ABOVE: In 1968 a group of NATO countries embarked on a programme to create a replacement for their F-104 Starfighter fleets. The Multi Role Combat Aircraft (MRCA) emerged as a swing-wing, twin-engined design employing engines developed by a consortium of Rolls-Royce, MTU and Fiat. Britain joined the programme in 1968 and the Netherlands and Canada later withdrew. The prototype MRCA (illustrated) first flew on 14 August 1974 from Manching, and Germany purchased 247 aircraft, the first entering service in July 1979. The Luftwaffe Tornado IDS fleet has been upgraded with new systems and weapons capabilities.

BELOW: Designed as a replacement for the RAF's Gnat and Hunter trainers, 175 Hawker Siddeley HS.112s were ordered in 1972. Originally named 'Tercel', the RAF opted for the more generic name 'Hawk' and the aircraft entered service in April 1976. Deliveries of a more advanced Hawk T.2, with an advanced cockpit and uprated engine, will see the RAF begin to replace gradually its first generation of Hawks from 2010 onwards.

BAe Hawk 21 August 1974

Panavia Tornado IDS (UK) 30 October 1974

ABOVE: The Panavia Tornado emerged from the multi-national MRCA (Multi Role Combat Aircraft) programme in 1968. It was eventually produced by a tripartite consortium consisting of British Aerospace, MBB (West Germany) and Aeritalia (Italy). The first production Tornado GR.1 was delivered to the RAF in June 1976 and was followed by the GR.1A, a dual-role ground- attack and reconnaissance variant with built-in sensors. The GR.1B, delivered from 1984, was a specialised maritime strike version of the Tornado, equipped with Sea Eagle anti-ship missiles. All variants were eventually replaced by the Tornado GR.4 and 4A (illustrated) as a result of a major update programme which began in 1996, incorporating new cockpits and systems including night-vision goggle capabilities, together with new weapons systems. Participating in both Gulf Wars together with other operations such as Kosovo, the Tornado remains at the forefront of the RAF's offensive capability and is expected to undergo another upgrade programme enabling the aircraft to remain in service until at least 2020.

RIGHT: The Hawker Siddeley Coastguarder was a specialised derivative of the Series 748 turboprop transport aircraft developed by Avro during the late 1950s (see page 130). The 748 emerged as two distinct designs, the short-haul passenger transport 748 and the military-roled tactical transport 780 which featured a redesigned rear fuselage incorporating a raised tail to accommodate rear loading doors and became the RAF Andover. Although export sales of 748 variants were good, British Aerospace (who took-over Hawker Siddeley) tried to increase sales by developing the aircraft for specific roles and the Coastguarder appeared in 1977, aimed at export customers requiring a low-cost maritime reconnaissance or SAR (Search And Rescue) aircraft. Little interest in the Coastguarder emerged and the 748-series was terminated, reappearing in the guise of the new ATP.

Hawker Siddeley Coastguarder
18 February 1977

BELOW: Naval interest in the Harrier can be traced back to 1966 when the planned construction of 'CVA-01' class aircraft carriers was cancelled. With fixed-wing flying expected to end in the 1970s when Ark Royal was decommissioned, the Royal Navy looked at a new, smaller carrier (referred to as a 'Through Deck Cruiser' in order to ensure funding) which could operate a navalised version of the RAF's Harrier. Some 57 Sea Harrier FRS.1 aircraft were purchased, the first entering service in 1978. Based on the RAF's GR.3 model, the Sea Harrier featured a number of design changes including a raised cockpit (giving better all-round visibility) and a Ferranti Blue Fox radar, giving the aircraft a more versatile capability which embraced ground-attack, reconnaissance and air-defence duties. Used to great advantage during the 1982 Falklands Conflict, the Sea Harrier was subsequently upgraded to FA.2 standard which gave the aircraft a new look-down radar, greater weapons capability and an improved cockpit. The update covered conversion of existing airframes and also included a batch of 18 new-build aircraft, all in service by 1999. Cost reductions led to the premature withdrawal of the entire Sea Harrier fleet in 2006 and pending delivery of the F-35, Harrier operations are now conducted as a joint operation with the RAF, using the Harrier GR.7/9.

Hawker Siddeley Sea Harrier 20 August 1978

BELOW RIGHT: The MRCA programme was geared towards the creation of a versatile ground-attack aircraft. However, the RAF also had a requirement for a new interceptor to replace Phantoms and Lightnings, and a derivative of the Tornado was developed specifically for this role, as a British venture, there being no requirement for such an aircraft for Germany or Italy. The basic Tornado airframe was retained but the fuselage was extended to house additional fuel and to provide attachment points for AAMs. The nose section was redesigned to accommodate a new AI radar, one of the two cannon being deleted and a retractable refuelling probe installed. The first

of 18 Tornado F.2 aircraft entered service in November 1984. Initial experience with the type was disappointing, but radar difficulties were resolved and 152 Tornado F.3s (illustrated) were ordered, with more-powerful engines and a better weapons capability. The first F3 entered service in July 1986. The aircraft proved to be an excellent weapons platform and the type has remained in use as new-built Typhoon fighters are introduced. The last squadron of Tornado F3s will stand down in 2011.

BOTTOM RIGHT: The Nimrod was selected for a second time as a Shackleton replacement during the mid-1970s when a decision was made on

the choice of AEW platform. The Nimrod was chosen chiefly because it was a British design and also because the radar system promised to be more effective than competing designs (such as Boeing's E-3). Flight trials began in 1982, and late-build Nimrods were withdrawn from the ASW fleet for conversion. The resulting aircraft was unusual with a huge fore and aft synchronised radar. Unfortunately, development of the radar proved to be a lengthy, troublesome and expensive business and in 1986 the MoD decided to abandon the programme and opted for a purchase of off-the-shelf Boeing E-3 aircraft.

Panavia Tornado ADV 27 October 1979

BAe Nimrod AEW 16 July 1980

BAe/MDD AV-8B (Harrier II) 5 November 1981

ABOVE: The unique capabilities of the revolutionary Harrier are inevitably attributed to British design expertise, however it's important to note that the original concept of swivelling engine jet nozzles was a French innovation, and that the Harrier could not have been completed without significant funding from the United States under the MWDP (Mutual Weapons development Program). Having successfully produced the early Harrier GR.1 design (and the equivalent US version the AV-8A), joint efforts were made to produce a second-generation Harrier (the AV-16) but the programme eventually failed and without British interest, McDonnell Douglas continued to explore the concept as a less-ambitious design which

ultimately resulted in the AV-8B (first flight made in November 1978), a much-improved version of the original Harrier with the same Pegasus engine but a completely redesigned airframe, giving the aircraft greater performance and much-improved weapons capability. British Aerospace rejoined the programme and the AV-8B was ultimately produced as a joint project, initial deliveries to the USMC in 1985 being followed by upgrades to night-capable versions and ultimately the Harrier II Plus with a new radar, enabling advanced AAMs to be carried. Export sales of the AV-8B were made to Italy (15 aircraft) and Spain (13 aircraft).

BELOW LEFT: The Firecracker was designed by Desmond Norman, co-founder of the famous Britten-Norman company. Created as a piston-engined basic trainer, it was anticipated that there would be a good export market for this inexpensive and capable aircraft. Subsequently, the design was refined into the NDN-1T Turbo Firecracker and three aircraft were produced for Specialist Flying Training who operated the aircraft for contract training of foreign students. NDN was renamed as the Norman Aircraft Company in 1985 and efforts to sell the Firecracker continued, but no sales emerged and with only four aircraft produced, the company went into receivership in 1988.

NDN Turbine Firecracker

1 September 1983

RIGHT: Given the great success of the RAF's experience with the Harrier GR.1 and GR.3, it was inevitable that a second-generation Harrier would eventually be procured. An initial joint programme between Hawker Siddeley and the US manufacturer McDonnell Douglas was abandoned largely due to cost overruns but MDD ultimately produced a less-ambitious redesigned Harrier, emerging as the AV-8B. BAe rejoined the programme during the 1970s and produced a British variant of the AV-8B. This was the Harrier GR.5, first flown on 30 April 1985. The later GR.7 first flew in May 1990 and became the RAF's 'standard' Harrier airframe. The GR.9 will probably represent the ultimate development of the Harrier design; the OSD (Out of Service Date) for the Harrier remains in question, and could be as soon as 2012, but the aircraft may remain in use by the RAF and FAA for many years more.

Britten-Norman AEW Defender 1984

ABOVE: The Britten-Norman Defender is a military derivative of the hugely successful Islander. Designed as a multi-role light transport, passenger and utility aircraft, the rugged and simple Defender has been sold world wide with more than 750 examples currently in operation and export sales (together with licence production) to more than 30 military air arms. In the UK the

Army operates seven Islander AL.1s whilst the RAF has three CC.2 and CC.3 aircraft. The Defender is a direct development of the Islander with a slightly enlarged airframe, optional piston or turboprop power plants and an ability to carry external stores on underwing hard points. Eight Defender AL.Mk.1 and AL.Mk.2 aircraft are currently in operation with the Army Air Corps.

One Defender was produced by the manufacturer to meet an expected market for a low-cost Airborne Early Warning (AEW) aircraft. Fitted with a Thorn EMI Skymaster radar set, the AEW Defender was offered to both the home and export markets and the demonstrator appeared at many shows. No buyers emerged for the aircraft and the project was dropped.

BAe/MDD Harrier II (GR.5/7) (UK) 30 April 1985

Embraer/Short Tucano 14 February 1986

LEFT: State-owned manufacturer Embraer embarked on the design of a new basic trainer aircraft for the Brazilian Air Force in 1978. A contract for two aircraft was agreed in December of that year, the first prototype flew for the first time on 16 August 1980, and 151 aircraft (the EMB-312) were produced for the FAB, designated as the T-27 in Brazilian service. In addition to basic training, 133 aircraft were produced to AT-27 standard, being employed as operational light-attack aircraft armed with a 12.7mm gun pod, bombs or rockets. Although basic in design, the Tucano is an agile and relatively fast performer, possessing jet-like handling, which has made the aircraft an attractive buy for a variety of export customers. These include Argentina (30 aircraft), Colombia (14), Egypt (54 with a further 40 produced under licence), France (50) and Iraq (80 produced under licence). The improved EMBH-312H 'Super Tucano' was designed to meet a USAF trainer requirement (subsequently given to the T-6 Texan II) but the aircraft formed the basis of the EMB-314 (the 'ALX') which is now in Brazilian service as the A-29. In the United Kingdom, Shorts entered into an agreement to produce the Tucano (as illustrated) under licence for both the RAF and for further export sales.

BELOW: Based on the familiar tandem-seat dual control Hawk trainer, the Hawk 200 was developed as an operational fighter-bomber for the export market. Built around a Northrop-Grumman AN/APG-66H pulse-Doppler X-Band multimode radar, the Hawk 200 features a completely redesigned forward fuselage and a single cockpit, together with a revised (taller) fin configuration. Twin Aden 30mm cannon are fitted into the nose and the aircraft retains the full weapons capability of its twin-seat counterpart, with a wider capability to undertake either ground-attack or air defence missions. Unlike other Hawk variants, the 200 can also be fitted with a bolt-on refuelling probe, giving the aircraft an excellent radius of action capability. Flying for the first time in October 1987, the first 200 demonstrator was lost in a tragic accident two months later. The aircraft has achieved modest export success, Abu Dhabi purchasing 18 aircraft in 1990, followed by orders from Oman, Malaysia and Indonesia.

BAe Hawk 200
19 May 1986

MDD/BAe TAV-8B (USA) 21 October 1986

LEFT: From the very beginning of the Harrier programme in the 1960s it was always envisaged that the single-seat operational Harrier would also be produced (in smaller quantities) as a twin-seat dual-control version. Handling the Harrier is a demanding task requiring the most able piloting skills and conversion onto the type from less-advanced trainers requires a dedicated trainer version in which both instructor and student can experience hands-on flying. The original Harrier GR.1 was quickly developed into the twin-seat T.2 configuration, although early RAF conversion onto the Harrier was conducted with only Hunter aircraft to use for flying experience (pending deliveries of the T.2), prior to making a first flight (and therefore first solo) in the Harrier. The USMC also took delivery of a twin-seat equivalent of its AV-8A. Following the creation of the second-generation Harrier (the AV-8B), a similar programme was initiated to produce a twin-seat derivative of the aircraft.

Short Tucano (UK) 30 December 1986

This emerged as the TAV-8B, essentially a 'standard' single-seat Harrier with a revised nose profile to accommodate a second cockpit, and a modified tail surface. The RAF received the Harrier T.10 (a direct twin-seat development of the GR.5) and this remains in service as the T.12 when brought up to the same standard as the Harrier GR.9.

BELOW LEFT: In response to a Royal Air Force requirement to replace the Jet Provost trainer, Shorts entered into a licence agreement with Brazilian manufacturer Embraer to produce the EMB-312 Tucano. This aircraft was selected by the RAF, and is now its basic trainer type, possessing good handling and agility which replicates (together with the cockpit layout) a fast jet environment for the student. Although essentially similar to the original Brazilian Tucano design, the Short Tucano T.1 features a more powerful 1,100hp Garret turboprop engine together with a strengthened airframe, new

cockpit layout (similar to the Hawk onto which students progress), a ventral airbrake, four-bladed propeller, a redesigned canopy, together with other minor alterations such as a revised oxygen system. Flying for the first time in this form on 14 February 1986 in Brazil, the first Shorts-built example took to the air on 30 December 1986. Deliveries to the RAF began in 1989 and the Tucano now equips No. 1 Flying Training School at Linton-on-Ouse, most aircraft wearing the markings of the component units, these being Nos. 72, 76 and 207 squadrons.

BELOW: Developed from the Hawk trainer, the T-45 emerged during the mid-1970s in response to a US Navy requirement for a new advanced trainer to replace the aged T-2 Buckeye and TA-4J Skyhawk. Manufactured as a joint programme between British Aerospace and McDonnell Douglas, the Goshawk first flew on 16 April 1988 and entered service with the US Navy in 1991. Although the aircraft was

intended to be a direct 'navalised' equivalent of the Hawk Mk. 60, the Goshawk was redesigned quite significantly for the US Navy, not least as a result of the requirement for aircraft carrier compatibility. The wing surfaces were redesigned considerably in order to improve the aircraft's low-speed handling, and the undercarriage was completely redesigned, being much stronger and featuring a twin nose wheel. A tail hook and fuselage-mounted airbrakes were also incorporated. More than 200 Goshawks are expected to enter service with the US Navy and are likely to remain in use until at least 2025. The T-45A will eventually be upgraded to T-45C standard with a new 'glass' cockpit, inertial navigation and other improvements. The T-45B was a proposed land-based version of the Goshawk, essentially an unmodified Mk. 60 aircraft, but this option was later dropped.

BAe/MDD **T-45A Goshawk** 16 April 1988

Eurofighter Typhoon (Germany) 27 March 1994

ABOVE: The Eurofighter Typhoon's origins can be found in Germany's TKF-90 concept developed in the 1970s. The German proposal for a delta-wing design with forward canards offered potential, and although British Aerospace rejected some of the more advanced features such as thrust vectoring, the design was adopted and proposed to the UK and German governments. France joined the programme in 1979 under the European Combat Aircraft programme but left after disagreements over project leadership, and ultimately Panavia (MBB, BAe and Aeritalia) produced the Agile Combat Aircraft design, combining British and German designs. After a long development programme, Eurofighter production orders were set at 232 for the UK, 180 for Germany and 121 for Italy, with a further 87 for Spain. German approval to purchase the Eurofighter was agreed in October 1997 and the Typhoon has now entered service with the Luftwaffe, gradually assuming air defence and some fighter-bomber roles currently undertaken by the aged F-4F Phantom.

Eurofighter Typhoon two seat (Spain) 31 August 1996

Eurofighter Typhoon two seat (UK) March 1997

TOP: When France pulled out of the Eurofighter programme, Spain opted to re-join the other nations leaving France to pursue its own design that emerging as the Rafale. Spain is expected to receive a total of 73 aircraft, these being assigned to air defence interceptor operations. As with all other Typhoon customers, a small proportion of the fleet comprises twin-seat dual-control variants, vital for conversion and continuation training.

ABOVE: The first Typhoon to enter RAF service was T.1 ZJ803 which joined newly formed No.17 Squadron on 30 June 2003. It was quickly joined by the T.1A, a twin-seat dual-control variant. The F.2 is the standard single-seat fighter variant. Later-production Typhoons will be the T.3 and the FGR.4, the latter representing the wider roles in which the RAF's Typhoons are expected to operate. Cannon armament and a full AAM and bomb-carrying capability will give the Typhoon a formidable multi-role capability for at least the next two decades or longer.

BAe Systems Nimrod MR.4   26 August 2004

ABOVE: A programme to replace the Nimrod MR.2P fleet began in 1992 and bids were submitted for a range of solutions including a variant of Lockheed's P-3 Orion, France's Atlantique and a British Aerospace proposal to redesign the existing Nimrod, creating a new 'Nimrod 2000'. The BAe proposal was eventually selected and this forms the basis of the new Nimrod MR.4 which will enter RAF service from 2011 onwards. Although retaining the same name and the same basic airframe, the Nimrod MR.4 is, effectively, a completely new aircraft. The original Nimrod fuselage has been retained (MR.2 aircraft being withdrawn from service and returned to the manufacturer for conversion), but in all other respects the MR.4 is a new-build aircraft with new wings, new BR710 engines, new systems and equipment and a new cockpit

layout, a great deal of the refit being derived from Airbus programmes. Cost-cutting has reduced the order for new Nimrods to just twelve, although the aircraft will provide the RAF with a more capable and reliable aircraft than the aged fleet of MR.2s. Likewise, the MR.4 is likely to be used for a variety of tasks in addition to the primary anti-submarine warfare role.

RIGHT: The Joint Strike Fighter is an American Lockheed Martin product. We have included it, because, as in the case of Airbus, this aircraft is a major international collaborative project. Of the programme's eight partner nations, the UK has made the largest contribution, in terms of investment ($2 billion) and workshare. The UK has two companies in "Team JSF", BAe Systems

which designed and produces among other things the aft fuselage, fuel system, horizontal and vertical stabilizers, and Rolls Royce, which has a 40% workshare in the F136 alternative F35 Lightning II engine and provides the Liftfan for all F35Bs. More than 100 British companies are involved, including Martin-Baker, Flight Refuelling and Smiths Aerospace.

Joint Strike Fighter 15 December 2006

2 Transport Aircraft

The story of the British aircraft industry's attempts to build successful transports and airliners in the post-war decades is a chronicle of a vain attempt to make up the huge gap that had opened at the end of World War II. At that time the US industry had a range of modern airliners such as the Lockheed Constellation and the more workmanlike, but equally efficient, Douglas range, including the DC-4 and DC-6. And, of course, there were literally thousands of DC-3s flooding the market as ex-military machines were sold at rock-bottom prices. Set against this background, Britain's initial attempts were feeble make-do bomber conversions such as the Lancastrian and Halton. The only transport in full production in early 1945 was the Avro York based on the Lancaster bomber. Almost all attempts to equal the American four-engined airliners were unsuccessful and the Avro Tudor and Handley Page Hermes were only built in small numbers while the more successful Vickers Viking was, in practice, little improvement on the DC-3.

Faced with this situation, the industry took some bold steps and produced two potential world beaters by taking advantage of their lead in jet and turboprop technology. The most successful was the Vickers Viscount, powered by four Rolls-Royce Dart turboprop engines, which took the world by storm and no less than 459 were eventually built before production ceased in 1964. A successor

was the much larger Vanguard but this only sold in small numbers. The other great pioneering aircraft was the de Havilland Comet, the world's first commercial jet airliner and one that appeared to have a great future when it flew in 1949. Initially, the company was swamped with orders and passengers enthused over the comfort and smoothness of the new jets. Unfortunately, two tragic crashes in 1953 led to the Comet's grounding and a major investigation highlighted some structural design defects. These were eventually rectified and the later Comet 4 inaugurated the first transatlantic jet passenger services in October 1958, only weeks ahead of the rival Boeing 707. Being later designs and benefiting from the lessons learnt in the Comet disasters, the 707 and the rival Douglas DC-8 quickly cleaned up in the long haul jet market – establishing a supremacy that went unchallenged for decades.

A contemporary of the Comet was the turboprop Bristol Britannia, which was late coming into service due to lingering problems with Proteus power-plants. By the time it entered service the glamorous jets were entering service and the Britannia again was only built in limited numbers despite its much better fuel economy.

The British response to the American jets was the Vickers VC-10, regarded by many as the most graceful airliner ever built but it suffered in the international

market by being too small as result of BOAC's insistence on hot and high performance for its Commonwealth African and Far East routes. The stretched Super VC-10 was a better prospect but was too late to challenge American supremacy.

Similar problems beset the short- and medium-haul markets. The graceful de Havilland Trident was originally too small due to the conservative requirements of BEA, the major British customer, and the market was monopolised by the similar, but larger, Boeing 727. After a shaky start with the loss of a prototype due to the hitherto unknown deep stall phenomena, the BAC-111 short-haul twin-jet airliner achieved a modest success but again was overtaken by an American rival, the Douglas DC-9, which built on the British experience. The last all-British airliner was the BAe 146 regional airliner developed from a Hawker Siddeley design of which over 350 were built in various guises before production was terminated.

Like military aircraft, the production of civil airliners became an international affair from the late 1960s and one of the greatest products of such programmes was the Concorde supersonic airliner. Unfortunately, this rather echoed the Comet story in that a great pioneering effort was initially rewarded with substantial orders but these gradually fell away in the face of the environmental objections to supersonic operations. Nevertheless, Concorde achieved a remarkable 30 years

BELOW LEFT: From Pioneers . . . the Comet was the world's first commercial jet airliner.

RIGHT: . . . to Partners. The Concorde was a brilliant departure from the norm, the only successful commercial supersonic transport, jointly developed by the French and British aviation industries.

of regular services with British Airways (BA) and Air France before being retired following the unfortunate accident at Charles de Gaulle airport.

Today the major British investment in large transport aircraft is through the Airbus consortium where the industry is a major subcontractor but no longer a partner following BAE Systems' sale of its share in 2007. However British industry still plays a vital role in the Airbus organisation, being the centre of excellence for wing design and production, and having a commanding expertise in the building of structures in lightweight composite materials. In addition many Airbus aircraft are powered by Rolls-Royce engines, notably the A380 where all initial production versions were British powered.

The next Airbus product to fly will be the A400M military transport which, although dogged by technical and production problems, promises to be an exceptionally versatile aircraft. With its wings being built at Bristol Filton and Rolls-Royce being a major partner in the Europrop consortium, the British involvement is considerable.

Seaplanes and Flying Boats

Historically Britain had relied increasingly on flying boats in order to expand and maintain air routes connecting the far flung parts of the British Empire in the period before the outbreak of war in 1939. There were many valid reasons for this trend, the most significant being that such aircraft could operate from any suitable stretch of water without the need for runways and other facilities required by land-based aircraft. Also, heavily laden conventional

aircraft needed progressively longer take off runs and it was realised that there was a limit to the potential size of an airport. The flying boat, on the other hand, could run for miles over stretches of water before gaining enough speed to lift the heavy load of fuel required for long-distance flying, quite apart from the weight of any passengers or cargo.

Before the war, the highly successful Short C class flying boats maintained regular services to the Far East and Australia whereas the later G class were intended for transatlantic services. The military version of the C class became the famous Sunderland, which played a vital role in defeating the U-boats. Towards the end of World War II, Shorts and BOAC began to look at peacetime requirements when it was thought that the flying boat would still be the primary long-range airliner. Already simple conversions of the Sunderland existed in the form of the Hythe, and after the war these were rebuilt as Sandringhams. In the meantime, an advanced version of the Sunderland, known as the Seaford was developed and this first flew in April 1945. However, it had only a limited service career, although the civil version known as the Solent served with BOAC until 1950. Subsequently, a few were operated by Aquila Airways until 1958 when British commercial flying boat operations finally ceased. Although Shorts were best known for the large flying boats, they did also produce the very attractive Sealand light amphibian, which achieved modest success in the export market.

The Sunderland and its derivatives were generally regarded as too small for

post-war commercial operations and in 1944 Shorts had flown the much larger Shetland. Much later, a civil variant commenced flight trials in 1947 but no production order was forthcoming. The ultimate British flying boat was the Saunders-Roe Princess, which was an entirely new post-war design and was powered by no less than ten Bristol Proteus turboprops. Intended to carry over 100 passengers (or 200 troops in a military version), the first of three prototypes flew in 1952, the largest British aircraft. However, by that time it was apparent that the future lay with the new generation of land planes then coming into service, especially as campaigns in World War II had resulted in hundreds of suitable airfields being constructed around the world, removing one of the flying boat's potential advantages. The other two prototypes never flew and were finally broken up after various schemes to utilise them, including a nuclear-powered option, came to nothing.

Saunders-Roe, of course, had a long association with marine aircraft and in 1947 flew Britain's first and only jet-powered flying boat. This was the remarkable S.R.A/1 jet fighter conceived for use in the Pacific War but by the time it flew the requirement had lapsed and the S.R.A/1 remained only an interesting diversion. By the mid-1950s the British aircraft industry had ceased to be involved in the design and construction of flying boats and a great tradition had come to an end.

Miles Aerovan 26 January 1945

General Aircraft Hamilcar X February 1945

Avro Tudor 1 14 June 1945

ABOVE LEFT: Frederick George Miles was famous as an innovative designer and the Miles Aerovan was one of his revolutionary designs. Miles' advertising described the aircraft as '...readily adaptable as freighter, 10 seat passenger plane, air ambulance, emergency operating theatre, flying caravan, mobile workshop, aerial shop or showroom.' A total of 51 Aerovans were constructed operating in East Africa, Belgium, Colombia, France, Holland, Iraq, Italy, New Zealand Spain, Switzerland, Turkey and the UK.

BELOW LEFT: Originally seeing service as the largest and heaviest glider transport used in World War II, the unpowered Hamilcar was in action during the Normandy landings and other theatres. The General Aircraft Hamilcar X fitted with two Bristol Mercury piston engines and strengthened structure was developed for operation in the Far East, but only 20 had been built by the end of the war and the type never saw action.

ABOVE: The Avro Tudor 1 was designed to a 1944 specification calling for an airliner capable of carrying 12 passengers in pressurised luxury over 4,000 miles, but in May 1947 BOAC rejected it on the grounds that it was incapable of operating a transatlantic service. Production of the Tudor 1 ceased and of the ten built, five became freighters, four were converted into Tudor 4s and one became the jet Tudor 8.

Vickers Viking 22 June 1945

In 1944 Vickers-Armstrong began designing the twin-engined, short-range Viking airliner. Its dimensions were similar to the Dakota, but it had 40 per cent more engine power and it could carry a maximum of 27 passengers. British European Airways was the largest operator and flew the first services in September 1946. The Viking was sold extensively and production ended in 1948 following the manufacture of 166 aircraft of which 66 were exported.

De Havilland Dove 25 September 1945

Short Sandringham 1 28 November 1945

LEFT: *Through its innovative design and ability to fill specific market needs as a small airliner, the de Havilland Dove was a success, first flying in 1945 with production continuing until 1968 with a total of 582 constructed and over 400 exported. It was bought by airlines, private companies and air forces alike. Its development was driven by the installation of increasingly powerful engines and higher operating weights, yet its overall dimensions never altered.*

ABOVE AND RIGHT: *The Short Sandringham was a long-range flying boat conversion of the military Sunderland. The nose and rear were reconfigured and the whole interior reconstructed with two decks, and accommodation for a maximum of 37 passengers. First entering service in 1945, a total of 18 were converted, with the last example flying until 1973.*

Bristol 170 Freighter 2 December 1945

The Bristol 170 Freighter/Wayfarer grew out of the need for a wartime military transport which could fly vehicles and supplies in and out of rough airstrips. The nose was fitted with clam shell opening doors for the loading and unloading of military trucks and hardware. Although it served as an airliner and civil freighter, more than half of the 214 built (174 exported) were initially delivered to air forces.

Handley Page Hermes 1 3 December 1945

Avro 19 (Anson) 30 December 1945

ABOVE: *In 1943 Handley Page set to work planning the Hastings, a large military transport aircraft, so a pressurised civilian counterpart called the Hermes, based on the same design became an obvious companion. The sole Handley Page Hermes 1, G-AGSS, crashed during its maiden flight on 3 December 1945 and as a result, development of the Hermes was suspended while Handley Page concentrated on the Hastings.*

LEFT: *The Avro 19 was a nine-seat civil airliner version of the military Avro Anson. Of the 56 Avro 19s built, the largest fleet of 14 was that operated by Railway Air Services, while the majority of the others served with British airlines, eventually retiring from airline use to become company communications aircraft.*

Avro Tudor 2 10 March 1946

LEFT: While the Tudor 1 was intended as a long-distance transport, the Avro Tudor 2 was 26 ft longer and designed to carry up to 60 passengers over shorter distances. The prototype flew in March 1946 but was found to suffer most of the aerodynamic troubles encountered by the Mark 1, so BOAC cancelled its order and the four Tudor 2s built were transferred to British South American Airways.

BELOW: The Airspeed Consul was a post-war civil version of the Airspeed Oxford trainer which could be either a six-seat airliner or a communications aircraft. It first flew in March 1946 and, in total, 161 were built including 46 conversions of Oxfords. The Consul saw service with small, scheduled and charter airlines in Britain, Belgium, Iceland, Malta, East Africa and Canada, and was the first type operated by Malayan Airways.

Airspeed Consul 15 March 1946

Handley Page Hastings 7 May 1946

LEFT: The Handley Page Hastings was a large, long-range transport aircraft which utilised a lengthened version of the Halifax bomber's wing with a new circular fuselage and a single fin. In service the aircraft was operated by a crew of five and could accommodate either 30 para-troopers, or 32 stretchers and 28 sitting casualties, or 50 fully equipped troops. The RAF received 145 and four were delivered to the RNZAF.

BELOW: The Miles Marathon was an 18-passenger feederliner whose development was taken over by Handley Page when Miles entered receivership in 1947. The Ministry of Supply had ordered 50 Marathons for BEA and BOAC, but these airlines rejected it, so 30 were delivered to the RAF as trainers and a few others saw brief airline use. A total of 42 were built.

Miles/Handley Page Marathon

19 May 1946

Short Solent 1 December 1946

Avro Tudor 4 9 April 1947

ABOVE: The Short Solent was a development of the famous wartime RAF Sunderland maritime patrol and attack flying boat. It had a stronger wing, larger tailplane and a longer fuselage, with accommodation for 34-44 passengers in a two-deck luxury layout. Production amounted to 23 and the major operators were BOAC, Aquila Airways and the New Zealand airline, TEAL.

LEFT: Following the rejection of the Tudor 1 by BOAC, ten Tudor 1s were completed as longer Avro Tudor 4s. Six of these were delivered to BSAA, but between January 1948 and January 1949 two Tudor 4s were lost in the 'Bermuda Triangle', and neither of these losses was ever explained. Following this, the Ministry of Civil Aviation relegated the Tudor to freight duties.

ABOVE RIGHT: In an attempt to rectify performance shortfalls one Tudor 2 was fitted with Bristol Hercules engines, replacing the Rolls-Royce Merlins, and was designated as an Avro Tudor 7 (seen here). Following tests, it was determined that the Mk 7's performance was no better than the Mk 2 and production plans were cancelled.

RIGHT: Percival Aircraft of Luton decided to develop a small airliner, the Merganser, at the end of the war. To keep costs to a minimum, it utilised components of the single-engined Percival Proctor and could accommodate five passengers and a crew of two. Only one Merganser was built, but it led to the development of the Prince which sold well.

Avro Tudor 7 17 April 1947

Percival Merganser 16 May 1947

Cunliffe-Owen Concordia 19 May 1947

Portsmouth Aerocar 18 June 1947

Vickers Valetta 30 June 1947

ABOVE: The Vickers Valetta was the military variant of the Viking airliner and had a strengthened floor and undercarriage, and double doors for loading. The 241 Valettas built for the RAF were used for passenger and troop-carrying, freighting, glider-towing, supply-dropping, navigator training and ambulance duties. The Valetta served from 1949 until 1968.

ABOVE LEFT: With the cessation of hostilities, Cunliffe-Owen sought to enter the civil airliner market with the Concordia, a 10-seat medium-range transport designed and built at Eastleigh in 1947. This airliner was of conventional design, with twin engines, a tricycle undercarriage and capacity for ten passengers. Two were built but as the aircraft could not compete with the many surplus DC-3s there were no sales and they were scrapped.

BELOW LEFT: The sole Portsmouth Aerocar made its maiden flight in June 1947 with 155 hp Blackburn Cirrus Major engines. It could accommodate one pilot and five passengers and was quite an advanced design, with a pod type fuselage, but the concept did not attract any orders and it was scrapped in 1950.

Airspeed Ambassador 10 July 1947

Design of the Airspeed Ambassador short/medium-haul airliner began in 1943. It was a high-wing pressurised aircraft with a capacity for 47 passengers, which flew in July 1947 but only entered service in 1953 by which time it had been outsold by the Viscount whose turboprop Dart engines gave it a major competitive advantage. As a result, production ceased after the construction of 23 aircraft with the final delivery in 1953.

Miles Merchantman 7 August 1947

ABOVE: On 7 August 1947 the sole Miles
Merchantman made its first flight, having been
designed, built and flown in ten months. It was
the ultimate development of the Aerovan design
and could carry approximately 2? tons of freight
or 20 passengers. Air Contractors ordered 20
with a conventional fuselage and 30 with a
detachable pod for freight transport.
Unfortunately the design was not put into
production owing to Miles' financial collapse.

RIGHT: The M.68 Boxcar was one of those clever
ideas that was never given the chance to come
to fruition. Based on the standard 50ft-span
wing and tail unit of a Miles M.57 Aerovan, the
Boxcar was powered by four 100hp Blackburn
Cirrus Minor engines and had a rear fuselage
fairing that could be attached directly to the
rear of the one-man cockpit, or relocated to a
position close to the trailing-edge of the wing.
The space behind the cockpit could then be used
to attach a 10ft-long road-transportable cargo
container, before the fairing was reattached. The
aircraft was capable of flying equally well, with
or without the container in place. Unfortunately,
the company ceased trading before the scheme
could be fully developed. The sole example of
the M.68 was scrapped in 1948.

Miles M.68 Boxcar 22 August 1947

Handley Page Hermes 2 2 September 1947

Short Shetland 2 17 September 1947

ABOVE: *Following the crash of the prototype Handley Page Hermes 1 on its maiden flight, worked stopped on the second prototype, G-AGUB. When work restarted, the aeroplane was lengthened by 15 ft and it was designated the Hermes 2 development aircraft. Some six months earlier in April 1947, the Ministry of Supply had ordered 25 examples of a further development – the Hermes 4 for operation on BOAC's African services.*

LEFT: *The Shetland, of which only two were built, was originally planned as a long-range reconnaissance flying boat but was reconfigured into a civil transport role instead. It had sufficient space to accommodate 70 passengers and 11 crew, but after the first prototype burnt out, no further development took place and the remaining Shetland never saw service.*

Short Sealand 22 January 1947

In January 1946 Shorts started work on a light, commercial amphibian aircraft for 5-7 passengers. The Sealand was a high wing mono-plane with a flying boat hull and both floats and a standard tail-wheel undercarriage; the two main wheels retracted into recesses in the hull. Even though only 25 Sealands were produced, 21 were exported and served in many parts of the world, including Bengal, Egypt, India, Indonesia, Norway, Venezuela and Yugoslavia.

Percival Prince   13 May 1948

LEFT: Following its experience with the Merganser, Percival created the larger and heavier Prince with more powerful engines and seating for twelve. 72 Princes were built (18 exported) for the Ministry of Aviation, Shell, Hunting Air Surveys, the Tanganyikan Government, Thai Air Force and a Swiss survey firm. The armed services of several countries also became customers, most notably the Royal Navy which used 48 Sea Princes for communications and training.

BELOW: On 12 July 1948 G-AHRF, the sole prototype Viscount 630 powered by Dart turboprops made its first flight. In July 1950 it received the first Certificate of Airworthiness for a turbine airliner and its smoothness, speed, pressurised comfort and large windows impressed passengers and airlines alike. This led to the development of the Viscount 700 and 800 series of which 442 were built including 356 for export.

Vickers Viscount 630   12 July 1948

Handley Page Hermes 4 5 September 1948

ABOVE: Successful testing of the Hermes 2 led to the Handley Page Hermes 4, the definitive production version, which differed primarily by having tricycle landing gear and more powerful Hercules engines. The first, G-AKFP, was flown on 5 September 1948 and was followed by 24 production aircraft. It had the distinction of being the first post-war British design to serve with BOAC.

RIGHT: The Armstrong Whitworth Apollo was a short- to medium-range airliner with accommodation in a pressurised cabin for 26-31 passengers and powered by four Armstrong Siddeley Mamba turboprops. Construction began of two flying prototypes in 1948 and the first flew in April 1949. However, the engine was prone to severe teething problems and with the success of the similar Viscount, further development was halted in June 1952.

Armstrong Whitworth Apollo

10 April 1949

De Havilland Comet 27 July 1949

The de Havilland Comet 1 made its maiden
flight on 27 July 1949 and it soon demonstrated
it could cruise at 490 mph at 40,000 ft carrying
36 passengers over 2,600 miles. In May 1952 a
BOAC Comet operated the first jet airliner
service, but two crashes caused by metal fatigue
temporarily ended the aircraft's progress. Some
Comet 2s served with the RAF but the airlines
had to wait for the Comet 4.

Handley Page Hermes 5 23 August 1949

ABOVE: Hermes development did not cease with the Hermes 4 as Handley Page built two Hermes 5 aircraft. These were the largest and fastest turboprop airliners of the day, but they were let down by the unreliable performance of 2,220 hp Bristol Theseus turboprops. Although versions of the Hermes 5 powered by other engines were considered, no further development took place and the Hermes 5 never saw commercial service.

Bristol Brabazon 4 September 1949

ABOVE: The Bristol Brabazon was the largest landplane when flown in 1949 with a 177 ft pressurised fuselage, 230 ft wingspan, and eight engines mounted in pairs but accommodation for only 100 passengers. However, it proved a 'white elephant' as the development of

turboprops and jet engines for airliners meant passengers could travel faster, above the bad weather and the Brabazon was, in contrast, uneconomical. Only one was completed and it was scrapped in 1953.

BELOW: The Scottish Aviation Pioneer prototype was underpowered but the Pioneer 2 re-engined with a 520 hp Alvis Leonides engine demonstrated excellent STOL performance and was ordered by the RAF which used the Pioneer extensively for tasks such as casualty evacuation during the Malayan Emergency, Aden and Cyprus. 59 Pioneers were built including 15 exported and it remained operational in small numbers until 1969.

RIGHT: The de Havilland Heron was an enlarged four-engined version of the successful de Havilland Dove, offering a rugged 14-17 seat airliner with Gipsy Queen 30 engines and a fixed undercarriage for short- to medium-range services into unsophisticated airfields. There were 52 Heron 1s constructed which were superseded by the Heron 2 with a retractable undercarriage.

Scottish Aviation Pioneer 5 May 1950

De Havilland Heron 1 10 May 1950

Blackburn Universal Freighter 20 June 1950

Vickers Viscount 700 Srs 28 August 1950

ABOVE: *Originally designed and built by General Aircraft as the Universal Freighter, when General Aircraft was taken over by Blackburn the prototype was dismantled at the Feltham, Middlesex factory and transported to Brough in Yorkshire for its maiden flight on 20 June 1950. Blackburn substantially developed it as the Blackburn Beverley for the RAF.*

LEFT: *BEA were impressed by the initial Viscount 630 but sought an airliner with greater capacity. The Vickers Viscount 700 with its longer fuselage, wider wingspan, modified systems and uprated Rolls-Royce Darts fitted the bill and the airline ordered 20. The 700 also impressed other airlines and orders soon flooded in from major carriers in Europe and around the world, so that eventually 287 were built.*

ABOVE RIGHT: *The one and only Auster B.4 G-AMKL flew on 7 September 1951. It had a four-seat pod and boom with clam shell doors for easy loading and unloading, and a four-wheel undercarriage was fitted. The fuselage floor had fittings for seats, cargo tie-downs, or litters for the air ambulance role. Although evaluated by the British Army, no orders were received.*

RIGHT: *The Bristol Britannia grew from a requirement in 1948 to produce a 32-seat airliner with a range of 1,500 miles, but the final design was developed to accommodate 90 passengers. The first prototype, G-ALBO, flew in August 1952 but the flight-test programme was badly delayed by problems primarily with the Proteus engines and the Britannia 100 entered service only with BOAC in 1957. Only 17 Britannia 100s were built.*

Auster B.4 7 September 1951

Bristol Britannia 100 16 August 1952

Saunders Roe Princess 22 August 1952

Percival Pembroke 21 November 1952

LEFT: *The only example of Britain's largest flying boat, the Saunders-Roe Princess flew in 1952. It was a 140-ton transatlantic machine with luxurious, pressurised accommodation for 105 passengers on twin decks with a range of 5,500 miles at a speed of 360 mph. Unfortunately, its ten Proteus engines performed poorly, adversely affecting its performance, and as BOAC was no longer interested in flying boats the project was cancelled in 1954.*

BELOW LEFT: *The Pembroke was a development of the Percival Prince civil transport which had its wings increased in span by 8 ft 6 in to permit higher operating weights. A total of 130 were manufactured from which 72 were assigned for export. It served with several air forces, most notably the RAF, which purchased them to replace the Avro Anson.*

BELOW: *On 14 December 1952, the de Havilland Heron 2 took to the air. In contrast to the Heron 1, it featured a retractable undercarriage, providing a 20 mph increase in cruising speed and a better fuel consumption. Of the 149 Herons built, 52 were Mk 1s and the remainder Mk 2s. 103 Heron 1s and 2s were sold for export.*

De Havilland Heron 2 14 December 1952

Bristol 170 Mk. 32 16 January 1953

LEFT: A special version of the Bristol 170 was the Mark 32 Superfreighter which had its nose extended by 5 ft and was fitted with 2,000 hp Hercules 734 engines. This was built for Silver City Airways and it allowed the airline to increase loadings on its cross-Channel ferry service, carrying 3 cars and 12 passengers or 2 cars and 23 passengers.

BELOW AND RIGHT: The Blackburn Beverley was a development of the Universal originally designed by General Aircraft. The Beverley had rear clam shell doors replacing the door and ramp, and the tail-plane boom was capable of seating 36 passengers. The RAF placed an order in 1952 and received 49 of the type renamed as the Beverley C.1.

Blackburn Beverley 14 June 1953

De Havilland Comet 3 19 July 1954

Handley Page Marathon (Leonides engines) 15 March 1955

Scottish Aviation Twin Pioneer
25 June 1955

LEFT: During the hiatus caused by the accidents that beset the de Havilland Comet 1, the sole Comet 3, G-ANLO, flew and took on the mantle of ambassador for the Comet, in addition to leading the flight development of the Comet 4. The Comet 3 possessed the classic look of the Comet but was enhanced by the 15 ft 5 in longer fuselage, providing a streamlined, elegant profile.

BELOW LEFT: Unlike all other Marathons which had four Gipsy Queens, the third Handley Page Marathon, which first flew in 1949, was powered by twin Armstrong Siddeley Mamba turboprop engines. In 1954 it became a testbed for the new Handley Page HPR3 Herald's engines and was re-engined with Alvis Leonides Major engines fitted in replica Herald nacelles. Following trials, it was scrapped in 1959.

RIGHT: The Scottish Aviation Twin Pioneer was a short take-off and landing aircraft designed with both civil and military operators in mind. It was conceived as a twin-engined version of the Pioneer. The prototype Twin Pioneer, registered G-ANTP, first flew at Prestwick Airport on 25 June 1955. Production ended after 87, including 33 for export, had been constructed, with the RAF as the largest customer operating a total of 39.

BELOW: The Handley Page Herald originated as a Douglas DC-3 replacement which could serve in rugged environments throughout the world, able to fly out of unsophisticated airstrips but transporting a viable payload. The designers chose a high-winged single tail configuration powered by four Alvis Leonides piston engines. Two prototypes flew in this configuration but were re-engined with Dart turboprops in 1957-8.

Handley Page Herald (Leonides engines)   25 August 1955

Vickers Viscount 800 Srs 27 July 1956

Bristol Britannia 300 Srs 31 July 1956

Percival President 26 August 1956

ABOVE LEFT: The Vickers Viscount 800 was built on the experience of the 700 but had a 4 ft fuselage extension and usable space increased by 9 ft. The 800 was best suited to shorter routes but it did have room for 71 passengers in a single class layout. The 800 led on to the 810 with higher-powered Rolls-Royce Darts and altogether a total of 155 Viscount 800/810s were sold.

BELOW LEFT: The Bristol Britannia 300 was a lengthened version of the Britannia 100 with passenger capacity increased to 114 and a similar version was delivered to the RAF as the 250. The final version, the 310, had greater range and stimulated interest from El Al, Canadian Pacific and Cubana and others who placed 37 orders for this quiet, sophisticated, long-range transport. Only 85 Britannias were built and 22 exported.

ABOVE: The development of the military Percival Pembroke led to the final civil version of the Prince, named the President which had higher operating weights and range than the Pembroke. Only three were built and these served in executive roles with the Ministry of Aviation and the British Aircraft Corporation.

RIGHT: The Miles HDM.105 was a variant of the Miles Aerovan modified with a Hurel-Dubois high-aspect ratio wing of 75 ft. It first flew on 31 March 1957 and the only example was registered initially as G-35-3, later becoming G-AHDM. It was employed on various trials until it crashed at Shoreham in June 1958.

Miles HDM.105 31 March 1957

Aviation Traders Accountant 9 July 1957

Handley Page Herald (Dart engines)
11 March 1958

TOP: The Aviation Traders Accountant was a turboprop airliner designed as a Douglas DC-3 replacement. It was powered by two Rolls-Royce Dart turboprops and first flew from Southend on 9 July 1957. The only Accountant, flew initially as G-41-1, but was soon re-registered G-ATEL. It was displayed at the Farnborough Airshow in 1957 but did not attract much interest and was scrapped in February 1960.

ABOVE: Handley Page decided to convert the Herald to twin Rolls-Royce Dart engines and the prototype, G-AODE, flew with Darts on 11 March 1958. The initial Herald 100 could accommodate 44 passengers, but following the fourth production machine, the aircraft was lengthened to become the Herald 200, providing accommodation for 50 passengers. The Herald proved only moderately successful and production ceased in August 1968 following the production of 50 aircraft.

De Havilland Comet 4 27 April 1958

ABOVE: The final Comet development was the de Havilland Comet 4 which, although built to the same dimensions of the Comet 3, had later Avon 524 engines. On 4 October 1959 BOAC Comet 4 transatlantic services began just ahead of Pan Am with its larger Boeing 707s. However for all the Comet's pioneering role, the Comet 4 achieved only 75 sales of all marks and the 707s substantially outsold it.

Armstrong Whitworth Argosy 8 January 1959

Vickers Vanguard 20 January 1959

LEFT: *The Armstrong Whitworth Argosy was a military and civil transport which first flew on 8 January 1959; a total of 56 were delivered to the RAF and 17 were built for civil operators. The civil version could be distinguished by its front and rear opening doors, while the military Argosy had the nose weather radome and the rear doors were changed to clam shell style with an integral loading ramp.*

ABOVE AND RIGHT: *With hindsight, it seems likely that development of a second-generation turboprop airliner should have been avoided. The Vanguard was a splendid aeroplane, and its Rolls-Royce Tyne engines were among the best powerplants of their kind ever produced. Its problem was simply one of timing. The design ran headlong into the faster-than-expected arrival of short to medium-range jets, and it could not compete with the speed and glamour of these newer airliners. The two customers that did buy Vanguards (British European Airways with 20 and Trans Canada Airlines with 23) certainly had good value: these 126/13- seaters operated on both sides of the Atlantic with remarkable economy.*

Avro **748** 24 June 1960

ABOVE: Following a major reduction in military procurement, Avro opted to rejoin the civil aircraft market and developed a transport design which had the potential to replace the ageing Douglas DC-3. The Avro 748 was a medium-sized turboprop airliner which first flew in 1960 and emerged as two distinct designs, the short-haul passenger transport 748 and the military-roled tactical transport 780 which became the Andover C.1 (see page 133). In a highly competitive market Avro concentrated on airfield performance and produced the 748 proved to be one of Britain's most successful airliners remaining in production until 1986.

Aviation Traders ATL98 Carvair

21 June 1961

ABOVE: *The Aviation Traders Carvair was devised as an inexpensive replacement to the Bristol Freighters used by the car ferry airlines from the late 1940s. It was a conversion of surplus Douglas DC-4/C-54s designed to carry cars with a new opening nose and a flightdeck raised above the fuselage. It proved far more financially viable than the Bristol Freighter and 21 conversions were produced.*

De Havilland Trident 1 9 January 1962

Vickers VC10 29 June 1962

De Havilland DH125 13 August 1962

LEFT: The de Havilland Trident 1 was devised for a BEA specification to carry 79 passengers in a mixed-class layout on short to medium ranges. This specification was not attractive to other airlines so the manufacturer heavily redesigned the wing for further marks as the Trident 1E, and later the 2E, to achieve further sales. Altogether 89 Trident 1s and 2s were sold which led onto the final version, the Trident 3B.

BELOW LEFT: The VC10 grew from a BOAC requirement for an airliner to service African and Eastern routes from airfields with short runways. BOAC was the main customer, and its VC10s entered service in April 1964. The other major customer was the RAF which received 14 fitted with a forward freight door and additional fuel tankage to increase range. In the 1990s these RAF aircraft were modified to provide and receive in-flight refuelling.

RIGHT: Following on from the great success of the de Havilland Dove, the de Havilland board gave approval for work to proceed on an executive jet replacement in March 1961. This proved a very sound move as in the intervening years more than 1,450 125s have been delivered and it remains in production, albeit now in the USA. The first production 125, G-ARYC, flew at Broughton on 12 February 1963.

BELOW: The Short Skyvan concept was influenced by the Miles Aerovan utility aircraft which first flew in 1945. Shorts built a low-cost aircraft of functional construction; with a square unpressurised fuselage allowing for rear-loading and a fixed undercarriage. The sole piston-powered Skyvan flew in January 1963, but as it was underpowered with Continental piston engines, turboprop Turbomeca Astazou 2s replaced them in October 1963.

Short Skyvan (Piston engines) 17 January 1963

BAC One-Eleven 20 August 1963

Short Skyvan (Turbine engines)

2 October 1963

ABOVE: *On 20 August 1963, the BAC One-Eleven 200 Series made its maiden flight with 60 orders from major airlines. The One-Eleven was designed as a Viscount replacement and was soon developed into the 300/400 series to operate at higher weights but with the same overall dimensions. Entering service in 1965, a total of 137 were built. A lengthened version of the One-Eleven, the 500 Series, flew in 1967.*

LEFT: *Turbomeca Astazous were introduced to replace the piston engines on the Short Skyvan in 1963 but when these proved unreliable they were exchanged for Garrett engines in 1967. The majority of Skyvan sales were for military or utility use and although it might not have won plaudits for its looks the concept was successful. When production ended in 1985, a total of 154 had been manufactured.*

ABOVE RIGHT: *A total of 31 Military Freighter variants of the Avro 748 was ordered by RAF. The aircraft had a longer fuselage and high tail with an air-openable ramp to allow for straight-in loading, unloading and aerial delivery. To hasten flight-testing of this variant, the first 748 prototype (pictured here) was re-engineered as the aerodynamic prototype of the Military Freighter, later called the Andover CC.2.*

BELOW RIGHT: *The Short Belfast was designed for an RAF requirement for a heavy-lift freighter to carry and air-drop a wide number of loads. These could include large helicopters, tanks or 200 fully-equipped troops. Only ten were ordered and served until 1977 when they were withdrawn owing to defence cuts. Five transferred to civil use and one is still flying in Australia while another is preserved at RAF Cosford.*

Hawker Siddeley Andover 21 December 1963

Short Belfast 5 January 1964

BAC Super VC10 7 May 1964

Britten-Norman BN-2 Islander 13 June 1965

BAC One-Eleven 500 Srs 30 June 1967

ABOVE LEFT: BOAC ordered 17 Vickers Super VC10s, a lengthened model of the VC10, and it also commenced transatlantic services in April 1965. The only other customer for the Super was East African Airways which received five. Nine of the Super VC10s (five BOAC and four East African) later flew with the RAF as flight refuelling tankers and five of these are in service at the time of writing.

BELOW LEFT: In more than 40 years of production, Britten-Norman has built 1,238 Islanders and Trislanders. The Islander was the brainchild of aeronautical engineers John Britten and Desmond Norman who commenced design in 1963 of a 10-seat STOL aircraft to replace the de Havilland Dragon Rapide. On 13 June 1965, the Prototype Islander G-ATCT made its first flight. In August 1967 the Islander received UK CAA certification and in December, US FAA certification.

ABOVE: BAC realised by the mid-1960s that demands for a stretched version of the One-Eleven were intensifying. BEA was also interested and as a result, the BAC One-Eleven 500 Series was launched in 1967 with an increased engine power and a fuselage stretch which allowed as many as 119 passengers to be carried. Major British and world airlines ordered 95 One-Eleven 500s.

RIGHT: In 1966 Handley Page launched the Jetstream, a pressurised, low-wing aircraft powered by twin turboprops capable of trans- porting 18 passengers and tailored to fill a gap in the feederliner market aimed primarily at the United States. Unfortunately Handley Page went into receivership in 1969, but the Jetstream was kept alive by interested parties who formed a company called Jetstream Aircraft.

Handley Page Jetstream 18 August 1967

BAC/Sud Aviation Concorde (France) 2 March 1969

The Anglo-French BAC/Sud Aviation Concorde
was developed to provide supersonic airliner
travel and initial forecasts indicated sales of
250-400. However between its maiden flight in
1969 and entry into service in 1976, the whole
climate changed and an increase in oil prices
and the universal banning of overland supersonic
flights meant that sales were crippled. Concorde
was a technical success but not a financial one –
only 20 were ever built.

Hawker Siddeley Trident 3 11 December 1969

Britten-Norman Trislander

11 September 1970

ABOVE: The Hawker Siddeley Trident 3 was the final manifestation of the Trident, specially developed for BEA and involving a longer fuselage providing accommodation for up to 180 passengers. Wing area was increased and to provide power for this much heavier aircraft the three Rolls-Royce Speys were augmented by a booster Rolls-Royce RB162 providing 5,230 lbs thrust for take off and climb. BEA received 26 and China two Trident 3s.

LEFT: Following the success of the Islander, Britten-Norman developed the Trislander with 18 seats by extending the fuselage fore and aft of the wing. The necessary additional power was found – unconventionally – by fitting a third engine to the vertical tail fin. Trislanders have served in airline service with operators worldwide and production continued until September 1984 with the completion of the 83rd Trislander.

ABOVE RIGHT: The first of a huge and continuingly successful brand of airliner, the Airbus A300 flew for the first time in October 1972. The A300 was designed to fill the gap for a wide-body medium-range airliner but orders were slow to come until Eastern Airlines of the USA placed a large order after which sales gradually grew. In fact the last A300, the 561st, left the factory only in July 2007.

BELOW RIGHT: Following on the success of the Skyvan, Shorts built an airliner development of the Skyvan with a longer fuselage more suitable to the passenger market – a 30-seater designated as the Short SD330 which flew in August 1974. It became popular as a short commuter airliner as did the military freighter version, the Short Sherpa purchased by the USAF. Production ended in 1992 following the manufacture of 140 aircraft.

Airbus Industrie **A300** 28 October 1972

Short **SD330** 28 August 1974

BELOW: *The Hawker Siddeley HS125-700 was a Garrett turbofan re-engining of the 125-600. The prototype, appropriately re-registered G-BFAN, flew on 28 June 1976. This new version, the 125-700, offered almost double the range while external noise was reduced to acceptable standards. It resulted in a spurt in sales and became the best-selling model with 215 sales until the advent of the 800.*

RIGHT: *In 1978 the newly formed and state-owned British Aerospace decided to re-launch the Jetstream 31 powered by the Garrett TPE-331. Building on their experience with the RAF contract the Jetstream 31 was produced at BAe's Prestwick plant (the former Scottish Aviation factory). The Jetstream 31 sold well and production ceased in early 1997 after delivery of 383 aircraft, more than 200 of which had been delivered to US airlines.*

BELOW RIGHT: *The sole Britten Norman BN2T Turbine Islander – G-BPBN which first flew on 2 August 1980 powered by Rolls-Royce Allison 250-B17C – was a conversion of a piston Islander which had originally flown in 1974. It was sold to a private owner in 1983 and scrapped in 1999. The Britten-Norman Defender (illustrated) is the very successful military version of the Britten-Norman Islander, specially adapted for military roles, it first flew in 1971. It had a specially strengthened airframe and undercarriage and could be employed as a utility transport, for casualty evacuation, counter-insurgency and light attack, maritime patrol, forward air control, patrol and reconnaissance.*

Hawker Siddeley HS125-700 28 June 1976

BAe Jetstream 31 28 March 1980

Britten-Norman BN-2T Turbine Islander 2 August 1980

Short 360 1 June 1981

ABOVE: This Short 360 was a stretched version of the Short 330 with accommodation for 36 passengers. The 360 differed from the 330 by the replacement of its twin fins and rudders by a new single swept tail fin. A fuselage plug was inserted forward of the wings, but the changed lines of the aft fuselage increased the internal length of the cabin. The SD-360 sold well and 165 were constructed.

ABOVE RIGHT: The BAe 146 was the product of design studies for a Dakota replacement which began in 1959 and finally resulted in 1978 in the launch of the BAe 146; available as the 70-88 seater 146-100 and 82-102 seater 146-200. The maiden flight of the BAe 146-100 was in 1981 and it entered service in 1983. The 146-100 and in its later refined manifestation the Avro RJ70 made total sales of 47.

BELOW RIGHT: The Airbus A310 is a medium/long-range, twin-engined, widebody airliner with a typical capacity for 240 passengers. It was launched in 1978, and was essentially a version of the Airbus A300 with a shorter fuselage and redesigned wing. Production of the A310 ended with the delivery of the 255th aircraft in June 1998.

BAe 146-100 3 September 1981

Airbus Industrie **A310** 3 April 1982

BAe 146-200 1 August 1982

LEFT: The total production of the BAe 146-200 (a lengthened version of the BAe 146-100) and its later improved version, the Avro RJ85, was 203 out of a total BAe 146/Avro RJ/RJX build of 390. The photograph shows four TNT BAe 146-200 QTs (Quiet Traders) – dedicated freighters with a large freight door fitted on the right of the rear fuselage.

BELOW: By 1980 the time was ripe for a major rethink in the 125's design. Hatfield's engineers devised the 125 Series 800 with many improvements including a greater wing span and American Garrett engines. In 1993 BAe sold the 125 programme to the American company, Raytheon, so development of the 125 passed to their hands. Approximately 860 125-800s have been sold.

BOTTOM: The ATP, later rebranded the Jetstream 61, flew in 1986 and was a much updated 748 which could accommodate 72 passengers. It became the victim of BAe's decision to combine in 1995 to form Aero International (Regional) with Aerospatiale and Alenia, to jointly market their aircraft. The decision was then made to end production of the ATP/Jetstream 61 after 65 were built as it would compete with the Aerospatiale/Alenia ATR42/72.

BAe 125-800 26 May 1983

BAe ATP 6 August 1986

Airbus Industrie **A320** 22 February 1987

BAe 146-300 1 May 1987

ABOVE: The Airbus is the best-selling Airbus model which competes against the Boeing 737. In mid-2009, Airbus delivered the 4,000th of its narrowbody Airbus 320 family which is available in different sizes, from the smallest – the A318, then the A319, the A320 and the largest, the A321. The A320, first delivered in 1988, pioneered the use of digital fly-by-wire flight control systems in airliners and serves with major operators throughout the world.

LEFT: The first BAe 146-300 flew in 1987. This development was achieved by stretching the 146-100 fuselage, but employing the standard engine and wing of the earlier series without seriously degrading airfield performance. Initially envisaged as a six-abreast 120-seater, it was re-configured in a 100-seat five-abreast layout for the regional airline market. Together with its improved late production version, the Avro RJ100, the 146-300 made sales of 142.

ABOVE RIGHT: BAe decided to exploit the 125-800 further and by introducing a 33-inch stretch to the fuselage married to the Pratt & Whitney PW305 engine, produced the BAe 1000 which flew on 16 June 1990. In contrast to the popular 800 Series only 52 BAe 1000s were built. Final assembly was not transferred to the USA and the final Hawker 1000 flew at Broughton on 18 March 1997.

BELOW RIGHT: Encouraged by the success of the Jetstream 31, BAe decided to develop the design further and launched the Jetstream 41 in 1989. The fuselage was lengthened to accommodate 29 passengers, powerful AlliedSignal TPE331 turboprops were installed as well as an increased span wing. Sales were subject to the vagaries of the North American airline market and in December 1998 BAe delivered its last Jetstream 41 following the constructed 104.

BAe 125-1000   16 June 1990

BAe Jetstream 41   25 September 1991

Airbus Industrie A340 25 October 1991

BAe (Avro) RJ85 23 March 1992

Airbus Industrie A330 2 November 1992

LEFT: The four-engined Airbus A340 is a long-range widebody airliner sharing its wing and fuselage design with the twin-engined Airbus A330. The A340 was devised for overwater routes where twin-engined airliners such as the Airbus A330 were severely limited. The A340 was available in four basic forms of which the A340-200 and A340-300 are out of production leaving the A340-500 and A340-600 still being built.

BELOW LEFT: The Avro RJ85 and the RJ70 and RJ100 were developments respectively of the BAe 146-100, 200 and 300. The RJ introduced digital avionics and an improved LF507 engine. To emphasise the improvements, the new aircraft were rebranded as Regional Jets, so each model would be identified by their passenger capacity with five-abreast seating: RJ70 (former 146-100), RJ85 (former 146-200), RJ100 (former 146-300). A total of 390 BAe 146/Avro RJs were sold.

RIGHT: The twin-engine medium/long–range A330 comes in two versions: the A330-200 and the slightly longer A330-300 with accommodation for approximately 250 to 300 passengers. There is also a military tanker/transport – the A330MRTT which has been ordered by the RAF and other air forces. By mid-2009, 630 A330s had been built.

BELOW RIGHT: The A321-100, which was the first alteration in the size of the A320 family with its 23 ft longer fuselage, flew in 1993 to increase passenger capacity to a maximum of 220. However owing to increased weights, its range was lower than the base A320 but Airbus redressed this by launching the A320-200 which has additional tankage and can carry a full load across the USA. The A321 has 768 orders.

Airbus Industrie A321 11 March 1993

Airbus Industrie A300-600ST Beluga 13 September 1994

LEFT: The Airbus A300-600ST Beluga is a grossly enlarged freighter version of the standard A300-600 widebody airliner especially rebuilt for the transport of Airbus parts to other Airbus factories as part of their assembly. They may also carry other non-Airbus freight. It first flew in 1994 and four more were modified at yearly intervals. However the parts of the largest Airbus, the A380, are too large even for the Beluga.

BELOW: The Airbus A319 is three frames shorter than the basic A320 and has a typical capacity for 156 passengers. It first entered service with Swissair in 1996 and was chosen by Easyjet which ordered 120 to replace its Boeing 737s. It is also available as the A319CJ Corporate Jet and the A319LR with longer range. 1,524 A319s have been ordered and the Airbus A320 family had received 6,418 orders in mid-2009.

Airbus Industrie A319 25 August 1995

Airbus Industrie A340-600 23 April 2001

Airbus Industrie A318 14 January 2002

ABOVE: The A340-600 is the largest of the four versions of the four-engined A340 with the greatest fuel capacity, a range of 7,900 miles and accommodation for 390 passengers. Now that overwater flight rules have altered, orders for the A340 have slowed considerably owing to the popularity of the twin-engined Airbus A330 and Boeing 777. Deliveries of all A340 versions amounted to 367 by mid-2009.

LEFT: The Airbus A318, designed for approximately 109 mixed-class passengers, is the smallest example of the A320 family and has had the poorest sales performance with only 83 orders by mid-2009. However the aircraft has just broken into the lucrative London City Airport market with its certification for operation from there and British Airways are offering luxury London City-JFK services with a spacious layout of 32 seats.

ABOVE RIGHT: The Airbus A380 is the world's largest airliner, larger than the Boeing 747. The A380 a double-deck, wide-body aircraft made its maiden flight on 27 April 2005 and entered service in October 2007. It is a phenomenal performer able to transport a maximum capacity for 853 passengers from the East Coast of the USA to the Far East. A380 orders total 200 and 35 had been delivered by mid-2009.

BELOW RIGHT: The A400M, which rolled-out in June 2008, is the result of a partnership between France, Germany, Italy, Spain, the United Kingdom, Turkey, Belgium, and Luxembourg, to build a four-engined military transport. Powered by four Europrop TP400-D6 engines and the eight-bladed Scimitar propeller, some 200 are on order.

Airbus Industrie A380 27 April 2005

Airbus Industrie A400M

Research & Development Aircraft

The decades following 1945 saw dramatic advances in aerodynamics and propulsion technology. The development of the turbojet as a reliable means of propulsion opened up new vistas for high-speed flight and much effort was devoted to the exploration of transonic and, subsequently, supersonic flight. Approaching the speed of sound, Mach 1, compressibility problems and shock waves caused major trim changes that were difficult to control, while the steep rise in drag required considerable aerodynamic advances to overcome it. To investigate supersonic flight the British Government sponsored the advanced Miles M.52 supersonic research aircraft in 1943 and by early 1946 it was almost ready to fly. Retrospective analysis of the design has showed that the M.52 would almost certainly have been able to exceed Mach 1 and some of its features were extremely advanced for the time and were subsequently incorporated in many other successful designs. Crucially the M.52 featured an all-flying tail plane that was shown to be critical in controlling the trim changes experienced in the transonic flight regime. Unbelievably, this promising project, which would have given Britain a commanding lead in supersonic flight, was cancelled on the whim of a government department in 1946. It was left to the Americans to make the first supersonic flight in late 1947 with the rocket powered Bell X-1, which also was fitted with an all-

flying tailplane but, unlike the M.52, was not capable of sustained flight.

The first British supersonic flight was achieved by the de Havilland DH.108 swept wing tailless research aircraft, which exceeded Mach 1 in a dive in September 1948. Unfortunately, the tailless configuration presented control difficulties and all three prototypes were destroyed in crashes, one of which killed Geoffrey de Havilland, son of the company's founder. This accident, and others, convinced the government that an incremental approach to the aerodynamic challenges of the day was the way forward and, consequently, an entire range of single-purpose research aircraft were subsequently commissioned. The mighty Vulcan bomber, for example, was preceded by the Avro 707 small delta-winged aircraft to investigate the characteristics of this wing plan-form, while the Handley Page HP.88, converted from a Supermarine Attacker, was flown to test the crescent wing configuration for the Victor.

The quest for a supersonic transport that resulted in the Concorde led to a number of research aircraft such as the HP.115, which was built to test the low-speed characteristics of the highly swept delta wing whereas the BAC.221 investigated the high-speed end of the flight envelope. The latter was developed from the Fairey FD.2, which had gained the World Air Speed record for Britain in 1956 – the first do so with a speed in excess of 1,000mph. One

field in which Britain did produce a genuine world-beater was that of the vertical take off combat aircraft and this had its origins in the Hawker P.1127, which flew in 1960. Much of the necessary work on control systems for jet-borne flight had already been done by Rolls-Royce on a bizarre-looking test rig aptly nicknamed the Flying Bedstead. In fact, the P.1127 was also predated by the Shorts SC.1 delta wing jet VTOL aircraft, which first flew as early as 1957, although full transitions from forward to vertical flight, and vice versa, were not achieved until 1960. In the meantime Shorts had already made themselves something of a name for producing research aircraft such as the tailless Sherpa in 1951 and the SB.5, built to test the low-speed handling of the highly swept wing intended for the English Electric P.1A.

Apart from the purpose-built aircraft featured in this section, numerous other aircraft were pressed into service to test engines, equipment and aerodynamic devices. Predictably, most of these were bombers or transports such as the Lancaster, Lincoln, Viking and Vulcan, which were large enough to be fitted with different engines and whose fuselages could accommodate test observers and their equipment. The routine tests conducted by these aircraft were vital to the steady progress that was made although space does not permit their inclusion.

Fairey Spearfish   5 July 1945

Built to meet a wartime Naval Staff specification (0.5/43), the Spearfish was designed as a replacement for the company's widely produced Barracuda torpedo bomber. Three prototypes were built (RA356, '360 and '363) but by the time the first of these had flown, the war was effectively over. An initial production order for 40 Spearfish TBD.Mk.1s was underway and the first of these (RN241) had flown before the order was cancelled. These big, Bristol Centaurus-powered, attack bombers were then allocated to various naval research and development units to assist in the proving of new weapons and techniques for naval warfare. At least one of them was reported to have been still flying with the Carrier Trials Unit at RNAS Ford until the summer of 1952.

Reid & Sigrist RS.3 Desford   9 July 1945

Although the RS.3 was not originally designed as a research aircraft, the sole example was later drastically modified to become the RS.4 Bobsleigh. The RS.3 was built as a private-venture trainer which could give both civilian flying schools and the military what the manufacturer would later describe as 'all-the-way' pilot training – presumably from the ab initio stages through to an advanced prospectus. Extensive development flying and demonstrations were conducted over the following three years, but the idea was not taken up and the aircraft was sold to the Air Council in May 1949.

Rolls-Royce Trent Meteor
20 September 1945

The first turboprop engine came about simply because Dr. (later Sir) Stanley Hooker of Rolls-Royce tried out a 10:1 reduction gearbox and a five-bladed propeller on the front of a standard Derwent turbojet. Conceived in 1943, the first engines were bench-tested in 1945. An early Meteor Mk.1 airframe was used for flight testing and EE227 (the 18th production aircraft) was modified by Gloster and Rolls-Royce. All weaponry was replaced by ballast; extra oil capacity was added for the gear-boxes, and extra fin area was provided on the horizontal tail. After a difficult start the flight test programme made good progress. The diameter of the five-bladed propellers was quickly reduced from 7ft 11in to 4ft 10in, and their available pitch range was drastically reduced. Although the RB.50 Trent was not developed into a serious production engine, the lessons learned during its test programme were steadily incorporated into the Dart – which quickly became one of Rolls-Royce's most successful and enduring powerplants.

De Havilland DH.108   15 May 1946

The three de Havilland DH.108s were built to gather detailed information on the behaviour of sharply swept wings at both low and high speeds. The data would be important nationally, but it would also be helpful to the Hatfield design office – busy finalising the new DH.106 (Comet) and DH.110 (Sea Vixen) designs. The DH.108s were all built to the same MoS specification (E.18/45): the fuselages standard Vampire FB.Mk.1 units taken from EE's production line at Preston; the tails, wings and Goblin engines adapted to their individual tasks within the research programme. TG283 was destined for slow-speed work and equipped with generous leading-edge slats and wing-tip-mounted anti-spin parachutes: TG306 and VW120 were both aimed at transonic research. Each was fitted with a progressively more powerful version of the Goblin engine. These three tiny machines added considerably to the sum of aerodynamic knowledge; one of them (VW120), became the first British aircraft to exceed the speed of sound. All three 108s were lost in fatal accidents: the slow-speed prototype failed to recover from a stalling test, while the other two both broke up at high speed.

Saunders Roe SR.A/1 16 July 1947

ABOVE: The Saunders-Roe SR.A/1 deserves its place in aviation history as the only flying-boat fighter produced by British industry. All through World War II, airfields had been vulnerable to enemy bombing and specification E.6/44 was seen as a way of overcoming this problem – especially in view of the island-hopping nature of warfare still being waged against Japan. Three twin-Beryl-powered SR.A/1s were built to examine the possibility of using such an aircraft – both in air-defence and ground-attack roles. Although the idea was good, the bulky flying-boat hull reduced manoeuvrability and turning radius to such an extent that the aircraft itself became vulnerable against the fast-developing land planes of the time. The whole concept was finally abandoned in 1950, but TG263 still survives at Duxford.

BELOW: During 1945 the Ministry of Supply issued Specification A.2/45, calling for a new Air Observation Post aircraft to replace the Army's battle-weary fleet of Taylorcraft-Austers. The Heston Aircraft Co. was one of two companies invited to build development prototypes. The delicate-looking JC.6 seemed an unlikely candidate for such rough-field operations, but its twin-boom pusher configuration, together with an overhung greenhouse-type canopy, gave the pilot and observer an unrivalled field of view. During the trials at Middle Wallop in 1948, it was noted that the JC.6 had a truly 'dismal' take off performance, and that alone would have disqualified it for the role.

Heston JC.6 (A2/45) September 1947

Hawker P.1040 2 September 1947

ABOVE: The P.1040 was Hawker's first jet aircraft and it was designed virtually as a private venture, with little more than general approval and 'interest' being expressed by members of the Air Staff. By October 1945, Hawkers had decided to build a prototype. It was not until

January 1946 that the Naval Staff saw it as a possible new interceptor and issued Specification N.7/46 to cover three prototypes and one test airframe. The first aircraft was not armed or operationally equipped in any way; it was simply an aerodynamic test vehicle. The first proper

naval aircraft (VP413) was fitted with a 5,000lb-thrust Nene 2 engine and most of the operational equipment, and went on to complete all the carrier trials on board HMS Illustrious The first Sea Hawk production airframe (WF143) flew on 14 November 1951.

Scottish Aviation A4/45 5 November 1947

RIGHT: During 1945 the Air Ministry called for a communications aircraft capable of operating into, and out of, confined spaces. The design submitted by Scottish Aviation Ltd had a remarkable wing that generated a quite sensational take off and landing performance. Despite its startling performance, VL515 did not make any real progress until its 250hp Gipsy Queen engine was replaced by the new 520hp Alvis Leonides radial. At this stage, with double the power, passenger capacity was increased from three to four, and the aircraft later developed into the popular Prestwick Pioneer.

Armstrong Whitworth AW.52   13 November 1947

ABOVE: Two of these graceful research aircraft were produced to meet specification E.9/44 – the first (TS363) was powered by two 5,000lb-thrust RB.41 Nene 2 turbojets, and the second (TS368) was fitted with the considerably less-powerful 3,500lb Derwent 5s. The idea behind the so-called 'flying-wing' configuration was to eliminate the drag associated with a normal fuselage and tail – a concept that had always attracted aerodynamicists because of its potential for increasing range and efficiency. The results from the AW.52 were disappointing, despite the use of laminar-flow principles to build the wing and advanced boundary-layer control systems to suck 'dead' air away from its surfaces. True laminar flow was never properly maintained and the aircraft failed to achieve its anticipated performance index. TS363 crashed in May 1949 after a severe case of flutter spread all across the wing, and TS368 was finally scrapped in 1954.*

Youngman Baynes High Lift

5 February 1948

LEFT: The MoS January 1947 order covered a full research programme based on a theoretical new wing and full-span slotted-flap system invented by R.T. Youngman. The wing was to be built separately and fitted to a proven design – the Percival Proctor IV. After being fitted with the more-powerful de Havilland Gipsy Queen 32 engine, the aircraft was nearly 3ft longer than a standard Proctor: the length of the main undercarriage legs was increased to provide clearance for the complex flap system, and the rear cabin was deleted to make room for a large electric motor that drove the flaps. At just 33ft, the wing was 42in less than the original, but it carried full-span primary flaps, attached to rear of which were a pair of half-span secondary flaps that moved to a steeper angle than the primaries, and covered the traditional gap under the fuselage. The large ailerons were attached to the primary flap sections, allowing them to maintain their relative angles despite the changing flap position. The whole system worked quite well, although the aircraft felt 'woolly' as the speed was reduced.

Gloster E1/44   9 March 1948

ABOVE: Following a wartime shortage of Rover and Halford jet engines for Gloster's twin-engined F.9/40 (Meteor) prototypes, the Ministry of Aircraft Production began to look more favourably on single-engined designs and issued specification E.5/42 to cover the possibility of F.9/40 being unreasonably delayed. The specification was reissued as E.1/44, and one of the Gloster submissions was accepted for prototype development. The first flight-cleared airframe was transported to Boscombe Down and flew during March 1948. Although its performance was satisfactory, its handling qualities were poor. Despite fitting a new tail on the second aircraft (TX148), the type was discontinued as not worthy of further development. The two prototypes continued flying for several years, as research 'hacks' at RAE Farnborough.

BELOW: The 107th Viking airframe was modified to meet a Ministry of Supply contract. There appears to have been no specific experimental requirement to cover the changes, but the aircraft was funded by the Government and certainly spent a considerable period conducting research and gathering data on the high- and low-frequency vibrations associated with turbojet powerplants. The airframe was converted during its initial construction, and the changes involved the fitting of two 5,000lb-thrust Rolls-Royce Nene 1 turbojets in place of the normal Bristol Hercules piston engines: parts of the wing, rear fuselage and tail were re-skinned with heavier-gauge material to cope with the acoustic battering they were likely to encounter from the jet engines, and the elevators were metal-skinned to protect them against thermal

problems. The engines were installed entirely under the original wing structure, which necessitated a novel four-wheel main undercarriage layout, with a single wheel on each side of each hand-made nacelle. The aircraft was used extensively in its research role, helping to develop the Nene engine, but also collecting data on such things as fuel consumption and sound-proofing at various speeds and altitudes. When its test-flying days were over, G-AJPH simply reverted to Hercules power and entered service with Eagle Aviation as a standard Viking 1B freighter.

Vickers Nene Viking   6 April 1948

Auster A2/45 28 April 1948

ABOVE: The Auster A2/45 was the second of two types put forward for development as the Army's new Air Observation Post (AOP) aircraft. Like its rival Heston JC.6, the Auster was powered by a 240hp Gipsy Queen 34 engine. The Auster was a little smaller overall than the JC.6 but it was still much bigger than any Taylorcraft or Auster type built before or since. Two aircraft were built (VL523 was flown nearly a year later than the first), and even the company's chief test pilot Ranald Porteous remembered them as having controls that were 'heavy, soggy and ill-harmonised' – unlike the Heston JC.6, which he also flew, and recalled as being 'crisp, light, responsive and well-harmonised' and 'infinitely nicer to fly'. The Auster was recognised as having a much better take off and landing performance, but still nothing startling, and only just missing the specification requirements. The aircraft were both extensively tested at Middle Wallop, but neither of them met the specification and A2/45 was allowed to lapse.

Avro Athena (Mamba engine)

12 June 1948

LEFT: The original Avro Athena design was built to meet a standard Air Ministry Specification (T.7/45) calling for a new, three-seat turboprop trainer to replace the Percival Prentice in its role as standard RAF trainer. Work was well advanced on two Armstrong Siddeley Mamba-powered prototypes (VM125 and VM132), and one Rolls-Royce Dart-powered example (VM129), when RAF Training Command switched its requirement to a new specification (T.14/47), calling for any future production aircraft to be fitted with the much cheaper and more readily available Merlin piston engine. This late decision left the three gas-turbine aircraft (now called Athena Mk. 1s), very much out on a limb and completely unrepresentative of the production model. In the event, the three Mk. 1s were retained by the Ministry for a brief period of use as development 'hacks' and pilot-familiarisation flying.

Avro Tudor 8   6 September 1948

ABOVE: The second prototype of the Avro Tudor 1 (G-AGST) – already modified to Tudor 4 standard – underwent even more radical surgery during 1948. The four 1,750hp Rolls-Royce Merlin engines were removed and replaced by new, twin nacelles, each holding a pair of 5,000lb-thrust Rolls-Royce Nene 5 turbojets. The Ministry of Supply needed an aircraft that was capable of long-endurance flights at high altitude, and recognised the Tudor as an ideal candidate. The Tudor 8 became the first airliner-style four-jet aircraft to fly in Britain – pre-dating the Comet by nearly a year. Despite its origins, the Tudor 8 was never actually configured as an airliner because its rear cabin was predominantly occupied by test instrumentation.

BELOW: The Hawker P.1052 fuselage was remarkably similar to that of the P.1040, but the new design incorporated a 35-degree swept wing. Two aircraft were ordered, both to be powered by 5,000lb thrust Rolls-Royce Nene RN.2 engines. These aircraft were the first examples of a fully pressure-plotted swept wing to be made available to the RAE. The second aircraft (VX279) was fitted with a variable-incidence tail in late 1949, but by March 1950 it was back in the factory for conversion into the P.1081. VX272 conducted a new series of high-speed trials, initially with an acorn fairing between both elements of the standard tail, and then with a completely new tail – fully pressure-plotted, of variable incidence and swept back to match the wing. In September 1953, the aircraft suffered a forced landing which led to its retirement.

Hawker P.1052   19 November 1948

Supermarine Type 510 29 December 1948

ABOVE: The Type 510 was the first step on an evolutionary path that would later lead Supermarine design teams to the Swift fighter. The Air Staff needed a high-speed jet fighter, and Specification E.41/46 was issued to cover construction of a swept-wing development of the earlier Type 392 Attacker airframe. Two aircraft were ordered, both to be powered by a single Rolls-Royce Nene 2 turbojet. Both prototypes originally retained the Type 392's tailwheel configuration, but the wing and tail surfaces were swept back by 40 degrees. All the early trials were flown with a blunt nose-cone but later modifications included a sharper nose to help the aircraft reach its specified design speed of 700mph. The second of these two prototypes (VV119) was flown later as the Type 528. (See separate entry.)

Handley Page Mamba Marathon
23 July 1949

LEFT: Construction of the sole Mamba-powered M.69 Marathon was under way when the company went into liquidation. It had been ordered by the MoS under specification 15/46 that called for a propeller-turbine version of the M.60 Marathon. BEA had expressed an interest, and the MoS suggested the 1,010shp Armstrong Siddeley Mamba as the primary choice of engine, with the Dart as a substitute. Handley Page Ltd absorbed Miles' Woodley assets and created a new company – HP (Reading) Ltd – to continue production of the piston-engined Marathon and complete the turbine prototype as the Marathon II. Tested in its proposed civilian role it went for military testing as VX231 and became the first turbine aircraft in the world to fly with reverse-pitch (de Havilland) propellers. BEA rejected the Marathon, and the programme was forgotten. VX231 re-emerged from the workshops in 1955 as the HPR.5, equipped with two 870hp Alvis Leonides Major radial engines in preparation for the HPR.3 Herald test programme.

Avro 707 4 September 1949

ABOVE: In its earliest form, the Avro 707 was seen as a straightforward, one-third scale flying model of the Avro 698 bomber proposal – later to emerge as the four-engined Vulcan. In fact, of course, the range of single-engined 707 variants that were to follow could never truly be described as scale models, but they were all closely linked, in one way or another, to the design and layout of the bomber. The first 707 to fly (VX784) was engineered to meet specification E.15/48, and was prepared as a slow-speed research vehicle, with the primary task of investigating any possible aerodynamic or control problems associated with the 698's delta-winged planform. Unfortunately, this first example was destroyed in a fatal crash less than a month after its maiden flight, and as a result gave very limited information to the overall research programme.

RIGHT: The second prototype of the original short-bodied Viscount 600-series was never completed with Rolls-Royce Dart turboprop engines. Instead, it was converted to become a dedicated test-bed for the new Rolls-Royce Tay turbojet, meeting the requirements of Ministry of Supply Specification 4/49. Its previously allocated civil markings (G-AHRG) were replaced by the new military serial VX217. The two engines were mounted under the wing in an almost identical manner to that used on the earlier Nene Viking – with a very similar, four-wheel main undercarriage configuration. The aircraft gathered much long-endurance data for Rolls-Royce, before being leased to Boulton Paul Aircraft Ltd, where it was very successfully used for the testing of power-control systems and components, particularly those related to the Vickers Valiant bomber. At the end of this second series of trials, the aircraft was declared surplus to requirements, and was broken up in 1959.

Vickers Tay Viscount 15 March 1950

Supermarine Type 528   27 March 1950

ABOVE: This was the second development aircraft built under specification E.41/46. A companion aircraft to the Type 510 (VV106) – and initially very similar to it – VV119 emerged from the factory with the sharper nose profile that would later be retrofitted to the first. After conducting little more than its own initial handling assessments, it was grounded for several months to undergo significant modifications. This airframe was about to be transformed into the Supermarine Type 535.

Hawker P.1081   19 June 1950

LEFT: The second prototype of the Hawker P.1052 was taken back into the workshops during early 1950, and converted into the new P.1081. The changes were done because the RAAF had asked Boscombe Down to evaluate the original P.1052 as possible front-line equipment. The scientists there recommended a fully swept tail and a more-powerful engine, which would need a straight-through jetpipe. The Rolls-Royce Tay was originally chosen, but because delivery of that engine was being delayed, the Nene was re-installed. The all-swept tail was, however, fitted, and the aircraft conducted a long series of trials that lasted until November 1950. The P.1081 was then handed over to the RAE for a planned series of test flights, but on 3 April 1951 it was destroyed in a fatal crash.

Supermarine Type 535   23 August 1950

ABOVE: *The tailwheel configuration of the early Supermarine jet aircraft (Types 510 and 528) was disliked by pilots, so VV119 was modified to bring it closer to a potential production-standard aircraft. The Type 535 was created by lengthening the forward fuselage and incorporating the nose-wheel layout (the tail wheel was retained, but only as an emergency tail-bumper). Another innovation was the fitting of a simple reheat system to the Nene engine, which needed a larger-diameter rear fuselage, and bigger intakes with slight changes to their lips: the rear tail cone was also 'pinched-in' to improve its gas flow. Other changes to the Type 535 included a slightly reduced sweep angle on the inboard section of the trailing edge, increasing wing area*

and giving the trailing edge its 'kinked' appearance. A number of other changes were made, most of them internal. After a series of positive flight-test results, an order was placed for two Avon-powered pre-production Swift prototypes (the Type 541s) and 100 production fighters for the Royal Air Force.

BELOW: *Although it gives every impression of being an early jet airliner, the Ashton was designed and ordered by the MoS purely as a research vehicle. Six airframes were built, and they became some of the most versatile and reliable test mounts available to British industry. Each aircraft was equipped with a pressurised crew compartment and much of the research*

work involved long-endurance flights at very high altitudes. They were allocated to various Government establishments according to their scientific needs, and several were shuffled around to take part in a wide variety of programmes. The underwing hardpoints variously carried fuel tanks, radar equipment, bomb containers and new engines. During their many years of entirely safe test flying, the Ashton fleet made a significant contribution to countless programmes. The basic aircraft were all powered by four Rolls-Royce Nene turbojets, but later programmes saw the aircraft carrying the Avon, Conway, Sapphire, Olympus and Orpheus.

Avro Ashton   1 September 1950

Avro 707B 6 September 1950

LEFT: *Like the ill-fated first 707, the 707B was powered by a single Rolls-Royce Derwent engine, drawing air through a large dorsal intake. The new aircraft was again covered by specification E.15/48, but was nearly 12ft longer than its predecessor and had a completely redesigned nose section. Final construction was delayed by several months following the inconclusive report into the accident to VX784. To avoid even more delay, it was decided to use main-undercarriage legs from an Avro Athena and the nose gear from the Hawker P.1052 – although the nose gear was modified later to improve the 707B's angle of incidence on take off. There were various other minor modifications, but the final design appeared to produce an aircraft of more than adequate stability, and much useful work was done by VX790 before it was finally transferred to more-general research flying at Boscombe Down, Farnborough and Bedford. It was finally struck off charge in November 1957 and used as a source of spares for the remaining 707s.*

Boulton Paul P.111 10 October 1950

LEFT: *Air Ministry Specification E.27/46 was written in late 1946 calling for two identical delta-winged aircraft to conduct a transonic research programme. Early in 1947 the same specification was redrafted and reissued to incorporate major changes to the second aircraft. A submission was accepted by Boulton Paul and the aircraft were flown as the P.111 and P.120 prototypes. The P.111 was a classic 45-degree delta which offered a novel solution to the (then) new problem of intake configuration. The designers opted for a horizontal-oval opening in the extreme nose of the aircraft, and provided a bifurcated duct to carry the airflow around the nose-wheel bay and pilot's compartment. This layout gave the fuselage a large cross-sectional area and limited the attainable Mach number to around 0.94. Later in its career, the aircraft underwent a series of significant changes, and four petal-type airbrakes were flush-fitted around the fuselage, immediately aft of the cockpit: in this new form, it was known as the P.111A. Although it never flew supersonically, it completed many years of useful research flying at RAE Bedford.*

Hawker P.1072 18 November 1950

RIGHT: After completing its significant contribution to the N.7/46 (Sea Hawk) programme, the Hawker P.1040 airframe was returned to Kingston and modified to take the lead in another research effort. Mixed power (turbojet/rocket) interceptors had been more than a passing interest to Government scientists since the late 1940s. When Armstrong Siddeley Motors Ltd started to have some success with its 2,000lb-thrust Snarler motor, the P.1040 was chosen to complete a series of flight tests. The aircraft underwent a major internal rebuild to accommodate a spherical pressure-vessel containing 75 gallons of liquid oxygen in the forward fuselage, and a separate tank in the rear to house 120 gallons of water-methanol propellant. The rocket motor was in the extreme rear of the fuselage, under the rudder, and liquid oxygen was supplied via an external pipe on the underside of the fuselage. Despite this major work, records suggest that the rocket was fired in flight just half a dozen times. By the very early 1950s, jet engines were being equipped with powerful and reliable re-heat (afterburner) systems, so rockets were less attractive.

Fairey FD.1 12 March 1951

ABOVE: In many ways the Fairey Delta 1 was one of the most remarkable aircraft of its time. Powered by a 3,600lb-thrust Rolls-Royce Derwent engine, this tiny machine had a wingspan of just 19ft 6in – some 10ft less than that of a Tiger Moth! It was built to meet the somewhat vague requirements of Experimental Specification E.10/47, which called for an aircraft capable of exploring 'revolutionary possibilities in the design and operation of fighter aircraft'. The earliest Ministry concept had foreseen a ramp- launched, rocket-boosted, vertical take off interceptor, that could protect capital ships at sea. Very little thought seems to have been given to the recovery of both the aircraft and its pilot after they had done their job, but the concept dictated both the size and layout of the FD.1. The vertical take off proposal was abandoned mid-way through construction, and the airframe was changed to meet the needs of a more orthodox research programme. After completing its manufacturer's trials, the FD.1 spent most of its time at Boscombe Down and Bedford, exploring the low-speed aerodynamics of a number of different flight-control and tail configurations. After an unpleasant landing accident at Boscombe Down in February 1953 (which destroyed the undercarriage and much of the underbelly structure) the aircraft was passed to the Proof & Experimental Establishment at Shoeburyness to end its days as a target for various explosive warheads.

Reid & Sigrist RS.4 Bobsleigh 13 June 1951

ABOVE: In 1949 the RS.3 Desford trainer was converted into a research vehicle to allow the investigation of the practical aspects of prone-pilot flying. Theoretically this would lead to a slimmer fuselage cross-section for high-performance jets, together with a reduction of the 'g' phenomenon that was causing pilots to black-out in high-speed turns. The original two-man tandem cockpit RS.3 was reduced in size, and everything forward of that was rebuilt to provide adequate space and extensive glazing for the experimental prone pilot. The aircraft was also fitted with Gipsy Major 8 engines and a new three-axis control-yolk in place of the conventional stick and rudder pedals. After its initial handling trials, it was delivered to Farnborough (as VZ728) in August 1951. The final research programme was over quickly: the new control yolk made the RS.4 almost impossible to fly accurately, and it lacked both the power and the airframe strength needed for high-speed turns. After languishing in a hangar for several years, it was stripped of its curious control-system and sold back into civilian life during January 1956.

BELOW: The third Avro 707 to fly was the first of two 707As (WD280 and WZ736). These were designed to investigate the high-speed end of the Avro 698's proposed limits and were far more representative of the bomber's final layout. The dorsal intake was replaced by wing-root intakes, and the dorsal fin was virtually doubled in length. The aircraft was still not fitted with power controls and its own speed was restricted to the 'highest possible subsonic speeds'. As a result, the 707As contributed less than expected to the bomber programme, but WD280 was later fitted with the compound-sweep leading edge that would be adopted for all production models of the Vulcan.

Avro 707A 14 June 1951

Handley Page HP.88 21 June 1951

TOP RIGHT: This one-off prototype was based on a mixture of component parts from a variety of companies. The aircraft was built to Specification E.6/48 and started life as a Supermarine Type 392 Attacker fuselage, partially modified during construction to an early Type 510 Swift standard. Feltham-based General Aircraft Ltd was given a contract to design and construct the unique crescent-shaped wing, the new tail assembly, and all the flying controls. After the merger with Blackburn Aircraft to create Blackburn and General Aircraft Ltd, the whole project was moved to Brough for completion under the Blackburn designation YB.2. The aircraft had been conceived as a means of gathering in-flight information on the wing and tail configuration being proposed for the Handley Page HP.80 (Victor) bomber. This picture clearly shows the new wing and tail layout, but before its first flight the HP.88 was painted midnight blue and given military markings with the serial VX330. Very early into the flight programme, it had been noted by pilots that aircraft suffered from longitudinal instability, which got worse as speed increased. Several small modifications were made, but the horizontal tail was still far too sensitive, generally leaving the pilot unable to 'catch up' with rapidly increasing oscillations. The HP.88 was flown to Stansted in August 1951 for a series of speed-calibration runs before its planned appearance at that year's SBAC display. During one of these runs, it seems that the problem reappeared with a vengeance and the aircraft broke up in flight, killing the Handley Page test-pilot Duggie Broomfield.

CENTRE RIGHT: Supermarine Type 541s, WJ960 and WJ965, were two pre-production aircraft ordered under Specification F.105. These followed-on directly from the Type 535s, but were powered by more-powerful Rolls-Royce Avon engines, in place of the Nenes fitted to earlier aircraft in this series. Despite their 'F' specification, the Type 541s were still development prototypes, and WJ965 (which was flown in July 1952) was far more representative of the final production aircraft.

Supermarine Type 541 1 August 1951

Short SA.4 Sperrin 10 August 1951

BOTTOM RIGHT: Although designed to a four-jet, Lincoln replacement specification (B.14/46), the S.A.4 Sperrin is here because the two prototypes (VX158 and VX161) were rejected as operational bombers in favour of the Vickers Type 660 (Valiant) proposal, and so spent their lives engaged in R&D flying. As originally flown, both aircraft were powered by Avon engines and their early trials concentrated on radar (and later visual) bomb-aiming systems planned for the fast-approaching V-force. Later, VX158 was fitted first with one, and then a second, de Havilland Gyron turbojet. After the Gyron's sudden cancellation both prototypes were scrapped by the end of 1958.

Supermarine Type 508 31 August 1951

ABOVE: At the time of its development, the Supermarine Type 508 was the most powerful aircraft ever designed to operate from the deck of a ship. It was the first in a series of twin-engined prototypes that would eventually lead to the operational Scimitar. The programme had its origins in the idea that a naval fighter would be better off without the weight and complexity of an undercarriage – operating instead from an 'accelerator/launcher' built into the carrier, and returning to a rubber deck or flexible 'carpet' of some kind. Supermarine had started work on this 1945 requirement under the Type 505 label, and had just received an order for six, when the Naval Staff cancelled the project and opted for a more rational approach. Supermarine was asked to continue with the 505 design, but this time with a conventional landing gear. Three aircraft were ordered under Specification N.9/47. This goes some way towards explaining the overall layout of the new Type 508.

Boulton Paul P.120 6 August 1952

Supermarine Type 529 29 August 1952

RIGHT: The Supermarine Type 529 was the second of three prototypes produced under Specification N.9/47. In essence, it was a more refined version of the Type 508, incorporating many of the lessons learned from its flight tests. Large rear-fuselage strakes appeared ahead of the V-tail, and 20mm Hispano guns were fitted in the forward fuselage. On both of these aircraft the rear fuselage tail-cone, carrying the V-tail, was movable over a 12-degree arc to act as a trimmer, and the hinged sections were operated in unison to act as elevators or in opposition to provide rudder control.

BELOW RIGHT: When a sharply swept wing was suggested for the RAF's first truly supersonic fighter (later to emerge as the Lightning) it was vital to understand more about the low-speed characteristics of the proposed layout. The original Derwent-powered SB.5 was designed to meet Experimental Requirement ER.100, which called for the equivalent of a low-speed Lightning – built to the same overall geometry, but aimed specifically at speeds below 350kt. The aircraft was unique because the wings and horizontal tail could be moved around – though not in flight – to create several different layouts on the same airframe, thus providing the best possible chance of finding a successful formula for the new fighter. The wing was designed to accept several different leading-edge contours and the geometry of the fixed undercarriage could be changed to accommodate any variations of wing-sweep or centre-of-gravity. After a highly successful experimental career, the SB.5 spent its final operational years providing valuable service to the Empire Test Pilots School at Boscombe Down: it was retired in 1968.

Short SB.5 2 December 1952

LEFT: The single Boulton Paul P.120 was the second of two transonic research prototypes covered by Air Ministry Specification E.27/46. Like its sister aircraft (the Boulton Paul P.111), the P.120 was powered by a single Rolls-Royce Nene turbojet, drawing air through the same design of horizontal-oval intake in the nose. The two aircraft shared an almost identical fuselage shape, and had very similar 45-degree delta wings. There were many internal differences, but the most significant external change involved the P.120's vertical tail. Whereas the P.111 was fitted with a simple triangular fin, the second aircraft was given a much broader-chord unit carrying an 'all-flying' (variable incidence) horizontal tail: the braking-parachute housing was also moved from its port-sided position on the P.111, to a new central position immediately beneath the rudder. It was thought that this new configuration would aid stability at high-subsonic speeds, but in the event the opposite was true. Only 23 days after its first flight, the P.120 developed a serious case of tail flutter while on a routine flight from Boscombe Down. The aircraft crashed not far from Andover and was totally destroyed, but the pilot managed to escape and parachute to safety.

Avro **707C** 1 July 1953

Short Sherpa 4 October 1953

ABOVE: The Avro 707C was simply a side-by-side, two-seat variant of the basic 707 research airframes. It was built to the same E.10/49 specification and to the same standards as the high-speed 707A machines. Two were originally ordered as pilot-familiarisation aircraft, but the second was cancelled before construction began. Although WZ744 taught a number of pilots about the idiosyncrasies of delta-winged flying, it had virtually no influence on the Avro 698 design. It spent most of its active life with the Royal Aircraft Establishment at Farnborough or Bedford.

LEFT: Shorts designed and built the Sherpa to test the aerodynamic qualities of a radically new 'aero-isoclinic' wing. This new layout replaced the traditional aileron and elevator control system with large, rotating wing-tips, which acted in unison to provide the elevator response or in opposition as the equivalent of ailerons. The aircraft was entirely funded by the company (with no government involvement at all), and it was thought that a much larger example of the new wing (114ft span) would later be applied to the design of an upgraded SA.4 Sperrin (the PD.1 proposal) as part of Short's bid for one of the V-bomber contracts.

Supermarine 525 27 April 1954

RIGHT: The third and final aircraft to fly under Naval Research Specification N.9/47 was the Supermarine Type 525. The contract had been amended in 1950 to allow VX138 to be built with swept wings and a cruciform tail, bringing it much closer to the operational layout of the final Type 544 Scimitar. The most important aspect of this aircraft was its new system of flap-blowing (or 'super-circulation' as it was then known). Based on the American Attinello blown flap, the system prevented flow breakaway over the flaps and considerably reduced approach and landing speeds. All subsequent aircraft in this series were fitted with the system and built under Scimitar production contracts.

Rolls-Royce TMR 'Flying Bedstead'

3 August 1954

LEFT: Early research done by the 'Flying Bedstead' gave Britain an unassailable lead in the race to develop control systems for VTOL aircraft. The TMR was little more than two Nene engines facing each other in a steel space frame. The efflux was driven vertically downwards from nozzles directly beneath the pilot's seat, and attitude control was maintained by an array of on-board sensors and four variable 'puffer-jets' built out on long arms. From the start, design responsibility for this project was shared between Rolls-Royce engineers and scientists from the RAE. It was never proposed to fit wings on the TMR and any transition to ordinary flight was obviously out of the question. The first tethered lift-off was made at Hucknall in July 1953 and the first free flight was achieved on 3 August 1954. A second machine (XK426) was flown free of tethers on 12 November 1956. The first machine was moved by road to Farnborough during January 1955 and then on to RAE Bedford on 21 June 1956, where it was joined by the more-advanced Short SC.1 during March 1957. The second TMR was due to follow XJ314 to Bedford, but during its planned final flight at Hucknall, it collided with the restraint gantry and crashed, killing the pilot. Only a couple of months earlier, the first aircraft had suffered an autostabilisation-system failure, which caused it to roll over and suffer damage. The Hucknall aircraft was wrecked, but repaired to static display standards and presented to the Science Museum in London.

English Electric P.1 4 August 1954

ABOVE: The two English Electric P.1s (WG760 and WG763) were built to Ministry of Supply Experimental Requirement ER.103 – issued in May 1947. They were both initially powered by a pair of non-reheated Armstrong Siddeley Sapphire 5 engines, mounted in staggered bays one above and behind the other. Almost everything about the P.1 design was disliked by engineers and scientists from Farnborough – the proposed 60 degree wing sweep was thought to be far too risky for such an important project, and the tail should be on top of the fin rather that low down on the fuselage. To prove their point, they even funded a new research aircraft (the Short SB.5) to collect supporting data. The SB.5 programme did at least show that the Warton team was correct all along. Despite all the doubts, the P.1 test programme made remarkable progress. The second aircraft flew on 18 July 1955, and later that year the Ministry placed contracts for three hand-built Avon-powered P.1B fighter-development prototypes, followed by the first small batches of five, and then 15, pre-production Lightnings.

Fairey FD.2 6 October 1954

LEFT: The Fairey FD.2 will almost certainly be remembered for its attack on the World Absolute Air Speed Record in March 1956. American aircraft had dominated this record for several years, culminating in the (then) current record of 822.26mph by a North American F-100 Super Sabre. The British aircraft beat that figure by no less than 310mph, and came away with a new record of 1,132mph! Despite these headline-grabbing activities, the FD.2 was designed as an aerodynamic research vehicle, and Experimental Requirement ER.103 was written around it. Two aircraft were built (WG777 flew during February 1956) and both completed several years of successful high-speed research and instructional flying at Boscombe Down and Bedford. The first airframe (WG774) was eventually converted into the BAC.221 (see later description) and taken into the Concorde development programme, while the second was retired after completing 429 flights, and moved comfortably into museum life. It can now be seen as part of the Cosford collection.

Armstrong Whitworth Prone Pilot Meteor   10 February 1955

ABOVE: The final stages of the prone-pilot trials (which had been started in 1951 by the Reid & Sigrist RS.4 Bobsleigh) were conducted by this much more suitable Meteor F.8. It had all the power needed, plus a strong airframe that would allow relatively high-g manoeuvres. WK935 was the last of a big production-batch of F.8s built by Armstrong Whitworth at Coventry, and it was converted there before delivery as a normal fighter. The extended nose was balanced by a larger tail-section from the Meteor Night Fighter line (in this case, a Meteor NF.12), which offered more surface area for greater stability. The forward cockpit was equipped with a normal canopy and windscreen, plus a small downward-looking panel immediately under the nose. The pilot lay face-down on a couch, in a semi-prone position, with his legs operating rudder peddles behind and below him: the small control stick was in front of him and operated in the normal sense. It seems that the forward cockpit had no heating system, because exceptional cold (and sore ribs) were constant factors in the pilot assessments. The trials were conducted on behalf of Farnborough's Institute of Aviation Medicine, and for the Bristol Aeroplane Company – which was planning to use the prone-pilot configuration for its Type 185 rocket-powered interceptor. In the event, the Type 185 was later cancelled, and the rapid development of personal 'anti-g' clothing and aircraft systems, made continued research into prone-pilot cockpits unnecessary.

M.L. Utility   August 1955

LEFT: In its earliest form, the inflatable-wing aircraft appears to have been an idea from of the Government's Research & Development Establishment at Cardington – indeed, an unregistered prototype is reported to have flown at RAE Twinwoods as early as March 1953. The Ministry of Supply ordered a batch of three development and evaluation machines from M.L. Aviation at White Waltham, in the hope that the aircraft might provide Army commanders with a light, cheap, reconnaissance and communications asset that could be deflated and packed into a Land Rover-type vehicle. All three of the underslung 'fuselages' were slightly different; twelve varied rubberised-fabric (similar to dinghy material) wings were constructed, with areas ranging from 390 to 530sq ft. Surviving records suggest that at least three different engines were tried. Despite this mix-and-match approach, and many hours of development testing at Farnborough and Boscombe Down, a successful formula was never really established and the programme ended without further sales.

Short SC.1 2 April 1957

Saunders-Roe SR.53 16 May 1957

ABOVE: *Three prototypes of the Saunders-Roe SR.53 were originally ordered, but one was cancelled before completion. The aircraft was a small, delta-winged, mixed-power interceptor fighter, built to meet Ministry of Supply Specification F.183D, and the much-amended Operational Requirement OR.301. The SR.53* was equipped with a tiny (1,640lb thrust) Armstrong Siddeley ASV.8 Viper turbojet, which was used for manoeuvring on the ground, for cruise and descent settings, and for generating electrical power. The Viper efflux was in the upper position, immediately beneath the rudder. All take-off and climb power was supplied by a controllable de Havilland Spectre rocket motor, which developed 8,000lb thrust at full throttle. The aircraft could not take off on turbojet-power alone, but the rocket propelled it from brakes-off to 50,000ft in a measured 2min 12sec.

Marshall MA.4 28 February 1959

LEFT: One of the most remarkable British achievements was the development of VTOL aircraft. The two Short S.C.1s (XG900 & XG905) were built to MoS Specification ER.143, which called for an aircraft that could take off vertically, transition into fully wing-supported flight for the cruise (with the lift engines shut down), and then decelerate to zero forward speed before landing vertically under full control, using jet power alone. Each aircraft was equipped with five specially designed RB.108 engines – each with 2,000lb static thrust and an 8:1 thrust/weight ratio. Four of these engines were installed vertically (on gimballed mounts that allowed fore and aft movement of 35 degrees), and the single propulsion engine was mounted at an angle of 30 degrees, in an S-duct below the tail fin. The first prototype S.C.1 (XG900) made its first flight as a conventional aeroplane (no lift engines installed) at Boscombe Down on 2 April 57. XG905 completed the first tethered hovering flight at Sydenham on 23 May 1958, and the first full transition was completed during April 1960.

BELOW RIGHT: Development of the vectored-thrust Bristol Siddeley BS.53 (Pegasus) engine gave airframe designers the chance to step away from research prototypes and concentrate on a VTOL combat aircraft. Politicians finally woke up to the idea that this was a promising programme, and in October 1959 agreed to fund at least the design work. Experimental Requirement ER.204D was presented to Hawkers in February 1960, and an order for two flying and one static test airframes followed in June – by which time, the company-funded prototype was substantially complete. A few weeks later another four aircraft were added to the same contract. The first aircraft (XP831) was powered by a flight-cleared, but still very unpromising, 10,400lb-thrust Pegasus 1. In order to complete its first tethered-hovering trials with this restricted thrust, the airframe had to be stripped of all non-essential weight. These trials began on 21 October 1960. The first free hover was achieved on 19 November 1960, after which XP831 was re-engined with a 12,000lb-thrust Pegasus 2, before beginning flight trials at RAE Bedford. The second of the two prototypes (XP836) was also powered by a Pegasus 1, and began its tethered hovering on 7 July 1961. The four follow-on development aircraft were fitted with increasingly powerful engines, up to and including the 15,000lb-thrust Pegasus 5. The next nine 'production' aircraft (ordered under a slightly later contract) were all semi-operational machines, built to a new designation as Hawker-Siddeley Kestrel F(GA).1s. These were used for field evaluation of the whole military VTOL concept, prior to the arrival of the first production Harriers.

ABOVE: During the early 1950s Cambridge University conducted research into the techniques of suction-based boundary-layer control, which required the removal of the very thin layer of slow-moving 'dead' air closest to the upper surface of a wing – thus reducing friction and improving wing efficiency. The MoA agreed to fund the project by donating an Auster T.7 airframe and paying for its conversion by Marshalls. The airframe was redesigned to meet experimental requirement ER.184D, and was fitted with an entirely new wing and bracing-strut arrangement, together with much bigger tail surfaces and a tougher undercarriage. A spin-recovery parachute was also mounted under the tail. The 40ft-span, high aspect-ratio wing together with the new tail surfaces were all plywood-covered, in place of the Auster's traditional fabric covering. The top surface of the wing was made porous, and air was sucked away by means of a small centrifugal fan driven by a 60shp Budworth gas turbine mounted in the rear of the modified cabin. The actual performance of the wing has never been released, but some reports suggest that the MA.4 was still controllable while flying at speeds as low as 30kts, and with an angle of attack of at least 38 degrees! After nearly 120 hours of very valuable research flying, the aircraft was sadly lost in a fatal accident during March 1966.

Hawker P.1127 19 November 1960

Handley Page HP.115 17 August 1961

ABOVE: The Anglo-French supersonic airliner (later to become the Concorde) was being designed around an incredibly slender delta wing, and both extremes of the proposed speed range needed considerable research before the final configuration could be frozen. The Handley Page HP.115 was designed to explore the slow-speed handling of such a wing, with particular emphasis being given to the Dutch-rolling characteristics, and to the generation of powerful vortices at high angles of attack. Because the aircraft was concerned only with low-speed flight, it was kept as simple as possible: the undercarriage did not need to be retractable, the engine (a 1,900lb-thrust Viper ASV.9) did not need to be powerful, and the movable flying controls could safely use Tiger Moth technology and be fabric covered. The upper wing surface was kept as clear as possible by mounting the engine on top of fuselage. The leading edges were easily detachable to enable different shapes and profiles to be investigated in flight. Two smoke generators were used to trace the vortex pattern over the wing, and the results were filmed from a position high on the fin. The HP.115 remained active with the RAE at Bedford for more than 12 years, making a massive contribution to our understanding of slender-delta aerodynamics.

Bristol T.188 14 April 1962

LEFT: The Bristol T.188 was one of the most advanced research projects undertaken by British industry. It was also one of its most costly failures. The far-sighted Experimental Requirement ER.134T was issued in 1952. It called for an aircraft capable of flying at sustained speeds in the region of Mach 3: the idea behind the programme was to investigate all the structural, thermal and aerodynamic problems that might occur at these speeds. The T.188 was built almost entirely of high-strength stainless-steel alloys and powered by two 10,000lb-thrust (14,000lb with re-heat) Bristol Siddeley Gyron Junior turbojets – always over-stretched in trying to push nearly 40,000lb of aeroplane and fuel up to its operational height, before a calibrated high-speed run could even be contemplated. In retrospect, the part of ER.134 that probably ruined the programme was the insistence on conventional take off and landing. While the Americans were making remarkable progress with air-launched research vehicles, the T.188 was forced to use nearly 70% of its available fuel just to take off and reach operational height, leaving little for acceleration, supersonic cruise and a safe recovery. Perhaps in-flight refuelling might have saved the project, but this simple technique was never tried. Two aircraft were flown (XF923, and XF926 in April 1963), but the maximum calibrated speed achieved before the programme was abandoned in 1964 was Mach 1.88.

Hunting H.126 26 March 1963

ABOVE RIGHT: Hunting Aircraft Ltd had been working for some years with the National Gas Turbine Establishment at Pyestock to develop a system of channelling combustion gases out over the trailing edge of an aircraft wing, thus creating the so-called jet-flap as a means of improving the lift coefficient and making an aircraft much safer to control at very low speeds. This curious-looking machine is the H.126, which was produced to meet Experimental Requirement ER.189D in order to research the principle. Up to 95% of the efflux from a single Orpheus engine could be directed into the wings to emerge as a thin, gaseous sheet over the top surface of the flaps. This stream would then follow the contour of the mechanical flaps and increase their area by forming a cascade of high-velocity gas behind the entire wing. Normal forward-propulsion nozzles were provided (just visible, low on the fuselage sides and to the rear of the main undercarriage legs) but these were fitted with thrust-spoilers to enable the pilot to control the proportion of thrust being delivered through the wing ducts. For control at very low speeds, the normal aerodynamic surfaces were supplemented by powerful gas jets in the wing-tips and extreme tail – similar in action to the familiar puffer-jets on a Harrier. XN714 spent most of its working life at RAE Bedford, but in April 1969 it was loaned for a year to the Ames Flight Research Center at Moffett NAS, in California. After returning in early 1970, it was retired by Bedford.

BAC.221 1 May 1964

BELOW RIGHT: At the end of December 1959, Experimental Requirement ER.193D was issued to conduct research into the high-speed properties of the unusual wing-shape being recommended for the Anglo-French Supersonic Transport – later to become Concorde. The first prototype of the Fairey Delta 2 (WG774) was taken into the Filton Division of BAC and rebuilt to incorporate the new ogival wing and all the associated data-recording and telemetry systems. To cover these modifications in detail, specification ER.221D was announced in July 1961. During the rebuild the engine was upgraded to an Avon RA.28 and the intakes were reprofiled and moved to a position under the leading edge of the wing. The fuselage length was increased by about 6ft, and all three undercarriage legs were made longer to provide a more flexible angle-of-incidence during take off and landing. The wing was fully pressure-plotted and a cine camera was built into the fin-top to record wool-tufting experiments. A new autostabilisation system enabled the pilot to pre-programme certain unstable conditions during the flight tests. The original 'drooping' nose of the FD.2 was retained, but the new version was made controllable, rather than limited to a simple up or down position. The remodelled aircraft flew during May 1964 and spent the major part of its productive life at RAE Bedford, working in conjunction with the Handley Page HP.115 to explore both ends of the Concorde flight envelope.

Dowty Fan Islander 10 June 1967

ABOVE: During the 1970s, Dowty-Rotol was keen to develop and market its new ducted propulsor system as a means of meeting a new stage of flyover-noise regulations. As a demonstrator and research aircraft, the company acquired a used Britten-Norman Islander (ex 5Y-AMU) and commissioned Miles-Dufon at Shoreham to handle the conversion. Both 300hp Avco-Lycoming piston engines were repositioned on pylons beneath the wing, and coupled directly to the propulsor units. These consisted of a 48in fan (instead of a conventional propeller) with seven variable-pitch aluminium blades running inside a profiled duct, carried on six downstream flow-guiding vanes. The front of the unit was fitted with a very large spinner. Trials showed a considerable reduction in both noise and vibration, plus an increase in the available thrust. The aircraft was restored to its original configuration in November 1983, after failing to attract any buyers.

BELOW: As part of the Nimrod AEW.Mk.3 development programme, an ex-airline Comet 4 airframe (originally G-APDS) was converted at Woodford to carry an early version of the forward-mounted Marconi Avionics radar antenna, together with a partial Mission System Avionics (MSA) kit in the fuselage. It was decided at an early stage that installing the proposed rear-fuselage radar was unnecessary. The Comet's original electrical-generating capacity, and its cabin-cooling system, were hopelessly inadequate for their research-flying task, so a new system was devised and installed in the rear fuselage. Despite its trials period continuing until mid-1980, problems with the radar system were never properly resolved. As soon as the first Nimrod AEW 3 was flying, XW626 was transferred to the RSRE at Bedford.

British Aerospace Comet 4 AEW 28 June 1977

Solar One   18 December 1978

2422
WORLD'S FIRST SOLAR POWERED AIRCRAFT

ABOVE: Solar-Powered Aircraft Developments was established by Mr Freddie To in order to work on a development prototype of Solar One – believed to be the first aircraft powered solely by energy from the sun. The airframe was designed to have all the characteristics of a glider, with an all-wood structure covered in an extremely light heat-shrunk plastic material. Power for the aircraft was derived from a solar array on the upper surfaces of the wing. This fed an electrical charge into 24 Ni-Cad batteries that were used to power four 0.75kW (1.0hp) electric motors, linked together to drive a 63in diameter, two-bladed propeller. The aircraft first got off the ground in a controlled 'hop' during December 1978. The first meaningful flights were conducted in June 1979: straight-line trips of more than 4,000ft, reaching a maximum a height of 80ft and speeds approaching 35 knots. The concept then, was proven, but 1970s solar-cell and battery technology were both severe limiting factors, as was the capricious British weather.

BELOW: During 1982 the British Government agreed to make a substantial funding contribution to an experimental aircraft programme (EAP) being put forward by BAe, and partners in Europe. One aircraft would be built, and its primary purpose was to integrate, in one airframe, many of the technologies that would be vital to future combat aircraft. For the first time, a canard-control configuration was used with an inherently unstable airframe – made possible by using a digital flight-control system. Several new materials and production techniques were used, including superplastic-forming of titanium components, metal-to-composite bonding, and an increasing use of carbon-fibre composites. The cockpit and on-board systems were also given considerable attention, with new fly-by-wire techniques. Although the aircraft was not designed as a particular prototype for the Euro-fighter, much of its technology was directly applicable

BAe EAP   8 August 1986

4 General Aviation

For the purposes of this book, the term 'general aviation' is applied to those smaller fixed-wing aircraft, mostly single-engined but including a few twin-engined ones, which were produced mainly for civilian use and have not been covered in other parts of this book. Prior to World War II Britain had a thriving light aircraft industry with such famous names as de Havilland, Miles and Percival. The industry was boosted in these years by government sponsorship of flying clubs and training organisations in order to build up a reserve of potential pilots for the RAF – an unusual example of forward thinking by the governments concerned.

After 1945 the outlook was initially bleak due to the scarcity and high cost of materials and an age of austerity in which few individuals could afford the perceived luxury of private flight. Gradually, the situation eased but the pre-war names were fading from the scene. De Havilland had become a manufacturer of advanced transport and military aircraft and although the company achieved outstanding success with the twin-engined Dove as a successor to the Dragon Rapide biplane, it did not again become involved in the civil light aircraft market. The delightful Chipmunk (designed by de Havilland Canada) achieved wide acceptance as a military trainer but experienced only limited civilian sales. Miles Aircraft were absorbed by Handley Page in 1947 and Percival

became part of the Hunting Group in 1944 and effectively ceased production of private light aircraft

Almost the sole major producer of light aircraft in the early post-war years was Auster Aircraft, which grew out of the war-time Taylorcraft Aeroplanes (UK) established to build the American company's designs in 1938. After being renamed in 1946, Auster built numerous variants in different configurations and constantly updated and improved the design, achieving major sales success both at home and overseas.

However, the writing was on the wall and from the end of the 1950s the British market was almost taken over by American imports, notably from Piper and Cessna, following the lifting of dollar-exchange restrictions. These manufacturers were producing strong, rugged and reliable private aircraft in quantities, which meant that prices were extremely competitive. In an effort to combat this tide, the assets of Auster and F.G. Miles were united to form Beagle (British Executive & General Aviation Ltd). Although some of the Auster designs were produced and improved, a major effort was made to introduce a series of new modern, all-metal aircraft to compete with the Americans. The results were the single-engined Beagle Pup and the twin-engined B.206 and B.242. Of these, the Pup was well received and sold in some

numbers, eventually metamorphosing into the Bulldog military trainer. The B.206 was less successful although some were sold to the RAF as the Basset and it did have the potential for further development. The B.242 was only flown in prototype form before the company failed and its assets broken up.

Since then there have been many efforts to revive the British light aircraft industry and several interesting aircraft such as the Trago Mills SAH-1, Richard Noble's ARV Super 2 and Edgley Optica have been produced but in every case the necessary financial backing to achieve full production has not been forthcoming. A notable exception is the Shaw Europa, which flew in 1992, subsequently selling over 1,000 parts kits before the company failed in 2004. However, the designer moved to America where an improved version is now in production.

The idea of homebuilt aircraft has often produced visions of Emmet-like structures taking to the air on a wing and a prayer. Today such an image is far from the truth and modern homebuilds, assembled from factory-produced kits, are often very sophisticated machines using the latest materials and technology. Unfortunately, few of these are of British origin but some examples are included here. Not included, due to reasons of space, are microlights and gliders.

Miles Gemini 22 October 1945

The twin-engined four-seater Miles Gemini made its maiden flight at the hands of G.H. Miles in October 1945 and was the last Miles design to enter quantity production at the Woodley factory in Berkshire. The Gemini proved extremely popular and 130 were constructed in the first year of production. Total production amounted to 154 of which 112 were sold abroad.

Auster J/1 Autocrat 20 November 1945

As the war drew to an end, Taylorcraft (later known as Auster) went ahead with the development of a tourer version of the Taylorcraft Auster AOP 5 observation aircraft. A prototype was designated the Taylorcraft Auster V Series J/1 Autocrat, but the type was more commonly known as the Auster J/1 Autocrat. The Autocrat was very successful and 420 were built.

Miles M28 Mercury 6 3 May 1946

Only one Miles Mercury 6 was built and flew at Woodley in 1946, registered G-AHAA, initially becoming the personal aircraft of the Chairman of British European Airways. There were six versions of the Mercury each slightly different from the other and designated as Mercury 1, Mercury 2, etc.

DHC 1 Chipmunk 22 May 1946

The de Havilland Canada Chipmunk was the first indigenous aircraft designed by the Canadian division of de Havilland. The Chipmunk prototype was registered as CF-DIO-X and is illustrated here on its maiden flight on 22 May 1946. It became the standard primary trainer for the RCAF, RAF and several other air forces during the immediate post-war years. Total production was 1,283 built in Canada, Britain and Portugal.

Auster J/2 Arrow Summer 1946

The Auster J/2 Arrow was designed as a successor to the pre-war Taylorcraft Plus C monoplane. It was a side-by-side, two-seater powered by an American Lycoming engine and first flew in 1946. However, British restrictions on the import of American engines resulted in 37 of the 44 aircraft built being exported. Most of those exported went to Australia. The aircraft photographed, G-AJAM, is one of the two surviving Arrows.

Chrislea Ace 7 September 1946

The prototype Chrislea Ace made its maiden flight in September 1946 and, unusually for its time, was fitted with a tricycle undercarriage. However it drew far more attention owing to its extremely unconventional manner of control. Instead of a control column there was a 'steering wheel' to control elevators, aileron and rudder. Only one was built as the production version was the Super Ace.

Newbury Eon 8 August 1947

Only one Eon, G-AKBC, was built by Elliotts of Newbury. It was a departure for Elliotts, who were glider builders, to build a powered aircraft and then it was decided not to press further with the project. G-AKBC crashed while employed as a glider tug. When the pilot swung the propeller in front of the unmanned G-AKBC, it moved forward pulling a glider with it through a hedge and writing them both off.

Chrislea Super Ace February 1948

The Chrislea Super Ace was developed from the Chrislea Ace and like the Ace had an unconventional 'steering wheel' arrangement instead of a control stick to control elevator, aileron and rudder. However, following severe criticism from flying clubs to whom it was demonstrated a conventional rudder bar was introduced. Only 17 were built including seven sold abroad.

Auster Model P Avis 22 March 1948

The sole Auster Model P Avis four-seater made its maiden flight in 1947 registered as Z-2 and appeared at that year's Farnborough Air Show. It received a Certificate of Airworthiness in 1948 but there was no further development and the Model P Avis was dismantled at Rearsby.

Slingsby T.29A Motor Tutor June 1948

The Slingsby T.29 Motor Tutor was a single-seat motor glider produced in 1947, by Fred Slingsby in Kirbymoorside, Yorkshire. Two prototypes (A and B) of the T.29 Motor Tutor were produced. Both of these versions flew successfully but there was considerable difficulty in certificating the aircraft with the Air Registration Board, which granted it a certificate only on the basis that it was not used for training, obviously precluding production.

Fairey Primer 22 October 1948

Only two prototypes were built of the Fairey Primer (the first is shown here) which flew in 1948 and was based on the Fairey Tipsy M. The second prototype was evaluated against the de Havilland Canada Chipmunk to become the standard primary trainer but was not chosen. Both prototypes were dismantled.

Auster J/5B Autocar August 1949

The prototype Auster J/5B Autocar G-AJYK flew in August 1949. A four-seater design that proved successful with 15 sales in Britain and 65 exported to more than 16 countries. Further versions of the Autocar introduced higher-powered engines to enhance performance, especially in warmer climes.

Chrislea Skyjeep 21 November 1949

The final manifestation of the Chrislea Ace and Super Ace was the Skyjeep which, in contrast to its predecessors, had conventional controls. It was designed to carry four passengers or freight. The prototype flew in August 1947 but only four more were constructed.

Luton LA4 Minor 1950

The Luton LA4 Minor was a two-seater high-wing monoplane built by Luton Aircraft and flown in 1939 but destroyed by fire in 1943. Post-war construction took place by a number of amateurs, the first known to have flown was G-AMAW in 1950. Production of an updated version for amateur constructors was begun by Phoenix Aircraft in 1958 and construction of 17 began, of which at least 12 were completed.

Auster J/1B Aiglet Summer 1950

The Auster J1/B Aiglet was essentially an Auster Autocrat with a Gipsy Major engine and a larger rudder. The Aiglet was intended for agricultural use and crop spraying but was also deemed suitable for normal passenger-carrying purposes. Most of the 86 Aiglets built were delivered engineless to the Antipodes where they were assembled.

Miles Aries 12 March 1951

In July 1951 F.G. Miles exhibited an improved Gemini known as the Aries at Hendon. The Aries had uprated Cirrus engines and strengthened structures. Only the prototype (initially registered as G-35-1 and later G-AMDJ) and one other Aries were sold, although three other Geminis benefited from some of the Aries refinements.

Britten-Norman BN-1 26 May 1951

The first aircraft designed and built by the innovative partners John Britten and Desmond Norman was an ultra-light, single-engined monoplane that flew in May 1951. Following an early crash it was re-engined and the wing span increased, but it was deemed unsuccessful and is now preserved at the Southampton Skyfame Museum.

Auster J/5F Aiglet Trainer 2 June 1951

Despite its name the Auster J/5F Aiglet Trainer had little connection to the Aiglet. Its fuselage was based on that of the Autocrat and with an improved wing was stressed for aerobatics. The prototype G-25-1 (illustrated here) first flew in June 1951 and when production ended in 1958, 119 had been constructed from which 91 were sold abroad.

Miles Sparrowjet 14 December 1953

The Miles Sparrowjet was a conversion of the prototype Miles Sparrowhawk, the first of five single-piston-engine racers built in 1935-6. In 1950 it returned to Miles at Redhill and was substantially remodelled as a twin-jet-powered racer. Its greatest success was winning the King's Cup race at an average speed of 228 mph in 1957. Unfortunately, it was destroyed by fire in 1964.

Somers Kendall SK.1 8 October 1955

The Somers Kendall SK.1 was a small tandem two-seat aerobatic jet trainer/racer. Designed by Hugh Kendall in 1954 for Nat Somers to compete in the National Air Races and built in a garage in Berkshire, it was first flown on 8 October 1955. The SK.1 suffered turbine failure in the air in 1957 which grounded it and it was never restored to fly again.

Auster B.8 Agricola 8 December 1955

The Auster B.8 Agricola's design originated from a marketing tour of New Zealand to assess agricultural transport needs. The resulting Agricola had a cabin with room for two passengers and also a tank capable of holding 144 gallons of insecticide. Unfortunately orders failed to materialise and only nine were built.

Edgar Percival EP9 Prospector
21 December 1955

The design of the Edgar Percival EP9 Prospector was influenced by Edgar Percival's market research in the Antipodes. The Prospector could carry six people or a combination of other loads such as oil drums or straw bales. Percival made the first flight of the prototype G-AOFU (seen here) in 1955 and carried out all the flight-testing. Production ended in 1961 after the manufacture of 47 machines which included 17 for export.

Thruxton Jackaroo 2 March 1957

The first Thruxton Jackaroo flew on 2 March 1957 and over the next three years 18 more followed. The Jackaroo was a conversion of the de Havilland Tiger Moth which entailed the fitting of a four-seat cabin instead of the original tandem open cockpit. Most served with the Wiltshire School of Flying at Thruxton.

Miles M.100 Student 14 May 1957

In 1953 the Miles brothers decided to build a prototype jet trainer which would be less costly to buy and operate than the Jet Provost, then being prepared for the RAF. Owing to Miles' limited resources when the Miles M.100 Student flew in May 1957 it was too late to be a contender for the RAF contract. Unfortunately the Student crashed at Duxford on 24 August 1989 but, at the time of writing, it is being repaired.

Rollason D.31 Turbulent 1 January 1958

The Rollason Turbulent was a factory-built version of the Druine Turbulent designed by Roger Druine. The Turbulent was designed to be amateur-built and was a single-seat, ultra-light aircraft with a low wing and fixed tailwheel landing gear, powered by a 1200cc Volkswagen or similar engine. Rollason produced 29 factory-built D.31 aircraft in the United Kingdom and three D.31A models with strengthened wings to allow aerobatics.

Auster J/1U Workmaster 22 February 1958

Only ten Auster J/1U Workmasters were produced. These were a development of the Auster J-1N of traditional high-wing layout, able to carry 90 gallons of spray fluid in a tank beside the pilot, an extra seat being provided for a passenger. The Workmasters were mainly operated in West Africa, three later returning and are currently on the UK civil aircraft register.

Farm Aviation Chipmunk 6 June 1958

In 1958 de Havilland produced two Chipmunks designated Mk.23s for crop spraying but did not proceed further owing to lack of orders. Two years later, Farm Aviation Services bought the surviving example and converted three others. The Chipmunks were heavily modified with a hopper tank in place of the forward cockpit for spraying duties. A small number of similar conversions were made in Australia by Sasin/Aerostructures.

Auster C.6 Atlantic July 1958

The Auster C.6 Atlantic had an undistinguished history and never even flew. It was designed as a four-seat executive tourer, a high-wing mono-plane with a tricycle landing gear. One aircraft, G-APHT, was built and its fuselage was displayed at the 1957 SBAC Show at Farnborough, following which development was abandoned.

Garland Bianchi Linnet 1 September 1958

The Garland Bianchi Linnet was a modification of the French-designed Piel Emeraude to achieve British certification. It was a side-by-side twin-seater light touring, school and club monoplane first flown in 1958. Two were built by Garland-Bianchi and then a further three by Fairtravel and known as Fairtravel Linnets.

Taylor JT.1 Monoplane 4 July 1959

The Taylor Monoplane flew for the first time in 1959. It represented the first post-war homebuilt design to emanate from England and was to be made in small spaces with the minimum of tools and material cost, requiring only average building skills from the constructor. The total number flying to date is greater than 110.

Auster D.5/160 10 January 1960

Auster produced three versions of the D series which had metal wing spars making them suitable for the tropics. The Auster D.5/160, a development of the Auster J/1N Alpha, flew in January 1960 and was a three-seater offering a choice of 160 or 180 hp engines. When Auster was taken over by Beagle in 1960, the D.5/180 became the Beagle D.5/180 Husky. A total of 211 were built including 170 constructed in Portugal.

Auster D.4 12 February 1960

The Auster D.4 was a twin-seater development of the J/2 powered by a 108 hp Lycoming. Auster Aircraft flew the prototype (seen here) marked with the Class B registration G-25-8 on 12 February 1960. A total of 41 was built of the type, including 9 assembled in Portugal by OGMA (Oficinas de Gereais Matereal Aeronautico).

Auster D.6 9 May 1960

The Auster D.6 was a four-seater – a development of the Auster Autocar available with a choice of two engines: 160 hp or 180 hp. When Auster was taken over by Beagle Aircraft in September 1960, development of the D.6 was dropped, while the D.4 and D.5 continued production. Only four were built.

Beagle A61 Terrier 13 April 1961

During 1959-60 Auster purchased a large number of Auster Mks 6, 7, and 10 from the British Army. These were re-manufactured on the Rearsby production line and offered in two versions; the Auster 6A and 6B. At the time of the completion of the first Auster 6B it was rebranded as the Beagle A61 Terrier. Production ceased after 64 had been built.

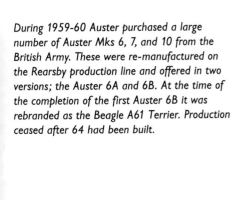

Beagle A.109 Airedale 16 April 1961

The Beagle A.109 Airedale was a four-seat, high-wing monoplane with a fixed, tricycle undercarriage based on the unflown Auster C.4 Atlantic design. The performance of the initial Airedales was poor largely due to their comparatively high structural weight. A weight reduction programme improved matters but it was unable to compete in the market and production ended after 43 aircraft which included the export of 18.

Rollason D.62 Condor May 1961

The Rollason D.62 Condor was a side-by-side twin-seater built at Croydon which first flew in 1961. Development continued through to the definitive version, the D.62B, which had a fuselage four inches shorter while some examples also had clipped wings with end plates, and all but the first four had flaps. Finally came the D.62C with a 130 hp Continental O-240-A which was followed by over 50 further machines.

Beagle 206 15 August 1961

The prototype Beagle 206X G-ARRM made its maiden flight on 15 August 1961 and a year later was followed by the enlarged Beagle 206Y G-ARXM, with accommodation for seven people. Production aircraft were further refined with higher-powered engines. The RAF received 20 and the type proved moderately successful. When the company needed space to build the Beagle Pup, production of the B.206 ended with the 85th aircraft.

Beagle AOP Mk11   18 August 1961

The Beagle AOP 11 was a three-seater military AOP (Air Observation Post) developed from the Auster AOP 9, and the prototype G-ASCC (seen here) flew in 1962. The Beagle AOP 11 was a high-wing monoplane powered by a Rolls-Royce/Continental engine. As no orders were forthcoming it was not put into production. G-ASCC crashed in 1995.

Beagle M.218   19 August 1962

The Beagle M.218 was an experimental four-seat, low-wing aircraft of composite light alloy and fibreglass construction. Only one aircraft was constructed. It was originally known as the Beagle-Miles M.218 and first flown by George Miles in August 1962 at Shoreham, initially as G-35-6 and later as G-ASCK. It was reconstructed as the Beagle B.242 prototype.

Isaacs Fury   20 August 1963

The Isaacs Fury was a 70 per cent scale replica of the 1935 Hawker Fury single-seat fighter. G-ASCM was the sole example built by John Isaacs in Southampton between 1961 to 1963 and flown at Thruxton in August 1963. It was later modified to become the Fury Mk 2 (as shown here) with a 125 hp Lycoming engine.

Clutton Sherry Fred 3 November 1963

The Clutton-Sherry Fred (Flying Runabout Experimental Design) was designed and built by E. C. Clutton and E. W. Sherry between 1957 and 1963 and is a single-seater homebuilt aircraft. It was first flown in 1963 and designed as a powered aircraft flyable by any experienced glider pilot without further training. Currently 25 are in existence. It is able to operate from small, rough fields and is easily transportable.

Beagle B.242 27 August 1964

The Beagle B.242 was an all-metal metamorphosis of the experimental Beagle M.218 G-ASCK capable of accommodating four people. Only one aircraft was constructed, registered G-ASTX, which made its maiden flight in August 1964. In 1967 Beagle decided not to develop the project further.

Luton LA.5 Major February 1965

The Luton LA.5 Major was a small two-seat aircraft built in 1939 by Luton Aircraft at the Phoenix Works in Gerrards Cross. The prototype was destroyed during a fire at the works in 1943. The rights to the design were obtained by Phoenix Aircraft in 1957 which adapted the design for amateur constructors.

Taylor JT.2 Titch 22 January 1967

In 1959 John Taylor designed and built a high-performance single-seater, the Taylor Titch, for amateur constructors seeking an aircraft faster than the Taylor Monoplane. The Titch first flew at Southend Airport in 1967. With a cruising speed in the region of 160 mph it can be used as an effective tourer and is also fully aerobatic. Builders can fit either a Continental or Lycoming engine.

Beagle Pup 8 April 1967

In designing the Beagle Pup the makers sought to produce an aerobatic twin/four-seater with the finesse of the American competition. The prototype twin-seater Pup 1 G-AVDF (pictured here) was first flown in April 1967. The 100th Pup was completed in September 1969. In December 1969 Beagle Aircraft was placed in receivership and even though 250 Pups were on order, production ceased after only 156 had been built.

Rollason Luton Beta 21 April 1967

The Beta was designed by employees of the British Aircraft Corporation at Luton for a racing aircraft competition in 1964. The design was then built by Rollason Aircraft and Engines and plans were made available as a homebuild. The Rollason Luton Beta was a wooden single-seat racer which made its maiden flight in April 1967. Betas proved successful air-racers in England during the late 1960s and early 1970s. Nine were constructed.

Mitchell-Proctor Kittywake 1 23 May 1967

The Kittywake was designed by Roy and Anne Proctor, with engineering support from Kit Mitchell, and was a homebuilt design aimed specifically at the sport/glider tug market. The prototype was G-ATXN, which was built as a homebuild project by the Proctors. The second and final aircraft, XW784/G-BBRN, was built as an apprentice training exercise by the Navy.

Sligsby T.66 Nipper 3 Early 1968

Developed by Avions Fairey in Belgium as an easy-to-fly, cheap-to-buy and maintain machine, the T.66 Nipper was a factory production or homebuild aircraft. Between 1959 and 1961 Avions Fairey delivered 59 aircraft and 78 kits. In 1962 Cobelavia assembled 18 Nippers. In June 1966 the licence was sold to Nipper Aircraft and 32 new aircraft were built by Slingsby Sailplanes until 1971 when Nipper Aircraft sold the licence.

Britten-Norman Nymph 17 May 1969

The Britten-Norman Nymph was designed and manufactured by Britten-Norman at Bembridge and flown for the first time in May 1969, registered G-AXFB (as shown here). It was intended to be bought in kit form for assembly by the purchaser. In 1971 Britten-Norman went into receivership and the Nymph was dismantled to save it from being scrapped.

Lockspeiser LDA 1 24 August 1971

The Lockspeiser Land Development Aircraft 1, G-AVOR, was first flown on 24 August 1971. This was a 'proof of concept' 70 per cent scale prototype aircraft described as an aerial 'Land Rover'. It had an unusual configuration, featuring a rear-mounted main wing mounted high on a box-like fuselage with low foreplane beneath the cockpit. While being brought up to production configuration at Old Sarum it was destroyed by fire in January 1987.

Practavia Sprite 16 June 1976

The Sprite was designed by a team from Loughborough University to meet a specification proposed by 'Pilot' magazine. The Sprite was a side-by-side, twin-seater, all-metal, low-wing, cantilever monoplane with a tricycle landing gear. It was powered by a Rolls-Royce Continental piston engine. Plans for amateur building were marketed by Practavia Ltd as the Practavia Sprite. A total of eight were built.

Scottish Aviation Bullfinch 20 August 1976

After Scottish Aviation took over the Bulldog trainer from Beagle following its collapse, the Bullfinch, a four-seat sports and touring version was developed. The prototype G-BDOG (seen here) flew on 20 August 1976 and within a month the first sale of a single aircraft was announced, but the company was unsuccessful in finding further customers. In 1977 Scottish Aviation was taken over by British Aerospace and the Bullfinch was cancelled.

Cranfield A.1 23 August 1976

In 1968 the British aerobatic team needed a single-seater aerobatic aircraft so Cranfield University students Bob Ward and Graham Potter designed the Cranfield A.1.
G-BCIT took to the air in August 1976, but its aerobatic qualities were not as hoped and so it remained a one-off. In June 1998 it was re-registered as G-COAI as the Cranfield A.1 400 Eagle and is currently stored by Cranfield University.

NDN Firecracker (Piston) 26 May 1977

In 1976, Desmond Norman, one of the founders of Britten-Norman, built the NDN Firecracker, a single-seat, piston-engined trainer designed to handle like a jet trainer. The piston-engined prototype flew on 26 May 1977. In 1983 three examples of a turboprop-engined version were also built. The type did not enter production.

Edgley Optica 14 December 1979

The Edgley Optica, designed by John Edgley, first flew on 14 December 1979. The Optica had an unusual configuration with a fully-glazed forward cabin seating three across, behind which was situated a Lycoming engine powering a ducted fan. It entered production in 1983. Companies producing the Optica have had an unstable history and production ceased after the manufacture of 21 machines.

Slingsby T.67 Firefly 15 May 1981

The Slingsby T.67 Firefly is a two-seat aerobatic training aircraft which has been used successfully by a wide number of air forces including the RAF and more than 250 have been built. It is of an all-wood construction, featuring a high aspect-ratio wing, reminiscent of a powered glider design. Unfortunately crashes while in service with the USAF resulted in their being withdrawn from use, but other forces continue to employ them.

NDN-6 Fieldmaster 17 December 1981

In 1981 Desmond Norman's firm built and flew the tandem-seat NDN-6 Fieldmaster which was primarily regarded as a crop-sprayer. In addition there was an oil-pollution clearance and fire-fighting version known as the Firemaster. In the meantime, NDN became Norman Aeroplane Company and five more Fieldmasters were built as NAC-6s. Plans for licence production of the Fieldmaster in Turkey were abandoned in 1999 after four aircraft were completed – two airworthy and two engineless.

Trago Mills SAH-1 23 August 1983

In the early 1980s Trago Mills built the Trago Mills SAH-1, with the intention of selling it to the RAF as a trainer to replace the Bulldog and it first flew in August 1983. The SAH-1 was rejected by the armed forces and, while five have been built in the intervening years, the rights to the design have changed hands several times.

NAC-1 Freelance 29 September 1984

Desmond Norman, who designed the Britten-Norman BN-3 Nymph, repurchased the Nymph prototype, G-AXFB. He reworked it as the prototype NAC-1 Freelance, now under the Norman Aircraft Company name, with an altered airframe, strengthened wings, re-located nose, new undercarriage and a 180hp Lycoming engine. The NAC-1 flew in 1984 registered G-NACI. However, orders did not materialise and only this prototype flew.

ARV Super 2 11 March 1985

Richard Noble, who won the Land Speed Record in 1983, recognised a gap in the market for an affordable, all-metal, side-by-side, two-seater light trainer. He set up a factory on the Isle of Wight to build an aircraft called the ARV Super 2 and the first prototype flew in March 1985. Later, production was transferred to Scotland and then Sweden, and when production finally ceased, 30 had been built.

Chichester Miles Leopard
12 December 1988

Two Chichester Miles Leopards were built and the second prototype, G-BRNM, is pictured here. The prototype first flew late in 1988 but it was grounded when the engine manufacturer went out of business. The second, improved prototype then flew with Williams International and a generally strengthened airframe. This is now at the Coventry Air Museum and the first aircraft is on display at Airborne Composites.

Shaw Europa   12 September 1992

Europa Aircraft is one of the most successful composite kit plane manufacturers in the UK, with the Europa XS Trigear, Monowheel and Motorglider acclaimed worldwide. There are over 400 Europas flying in 33 countries and many more in the build. The Monowheel and the Europa XS Trigear, with a tricycle undercarriage, are seen here.

5 Rotorcraft

The modern helicopter is a vital aviation asset in both civil and military activities, and today's machines with reliable engines, advanced avionics and stabilised control systems are capable of carrying out an astonishing variety of tasks. Although the pioneering Igor Sikorsky is generally regarded as the father of the modern helicopter, flying the VS-300 in September 1939, he had in fact been pre-empted by developments in Europe. Britain was already extremely experienced in rotary-winged flight through a series of autogyros, mainly through the efforts of the Don Juan de la Cierva, who set up his company in 1926. His designs were developed by G. & J. Weir Ltd resulting in the W.4 helicopter, which flew in 1938. As with so many promising lines of development, the onset of war delayed progress, although Weir took over the Cierva business in 1943 and started work on a number of projects including the massive W.11 Air Horse, which eventually flew in 1948. A more practical proposition was the W.14 light observation helicopter. However, by the time it entered production as the Skeeter in 1956 the Cierva Company had been taken over by Saunders Roe. The advent of the gas turbine provided an ideal power plant for helicopters and Saunders Roe developed the P531, which eventually saw service with the Army as the Scout and with the RN as the Wasp. Once again, though, by the time they were in service Saunders Roe themselves had been absorbed by a new entity, Westland Helicopters.

Two other major concerns had also taken up the challenge of developing helicopters in the post-war era and the largest of these was the Bristol Aeroplane Company, who flew their Type 171 Sycamore as early as 1947. The company, subsequently, built no less than 178 examples and although most of these went to military customers, a few were used by BEA for pioneering passenger and mail flights. The tandem-rotor Type 173 showed considerable promise in both military and civil versions but eventually only the turboshaft powered version saw service as the Type 192 Belvedere military troop carrier, entering service in 1961.

Perhaps the most exciting British helicopter advances were made by Fairey Aviation – starting with their unique Gyrodyne, which flew in 1947. Although lifted by a conventional rotor, its forward speed was augmented by two propellers mounted on short, stub wings. These gave additional thrust and, acting differentially, dispensed with the need for a tail rotor. The next stage was the so-called Jet Gyrodyne, which was in fact powered by a Leonides piston engine. However, this was geared to drive compressors that fed compressed air to the rotor tips where fuel-burning jet units were installed. This concept was tried on a much greater scale in the Fairey Rotodyne, a twin-turboprop convertible helicopter with a planned cruising speed of 200 mph capable of carrying around 50 passengers in the civil version. Although the prototype flew well, the project was allowed to die a death as both Fairey and Bristol were taken over by Westland in 1960.

In the meantime Westland had become the major force in British helicopters by the simple expedient of buying in foreign designs from Sikorsky. Starting with the S51 Dragonfly, Westland built British versions of the S55 (Whirlwind), S58 (Wessex) and S61 (Sea King). This policy was encouraged by the government in the 1960s although in this case attention turned to collaboration with France resulting in Westland building the French-designed Pumas and Gazelles. As part of the deal Westland also developed the WG.13 medium-sized helicopter for shipboard use and this was sold to the French Navy, as well as being sold in considerable numbers to other overseas customers. Subsequently, international cooperation has been the only way forward with Westland forming part of the EHI syndicate to design and build the EH.101 Merlin. This has proved to be a highly successful machine, even winning orders from the US for use as a Presidential transport. However, in the process Westland have all but lost their identity, now being part of the Italian Finmeccanica Group, although the production facilities remain at Yeovil in the UK.

Inevitably, this survey has concentrated on the major constructors but the simpler autogyro continues to have its adherents – notably Wing Commander Ken Wallis who has produced a whole series, some of which have become familiar through appearances in various James Bond films! Others have produced licence-built versions of American designs and autogyros remain popular due to their relative simplicity and small storage requirements when the rotors are folded. On the other hand, due to the complexity of the true helicopter, there have been relatively few built and flown by private concerns although one or two are illustrated in the following review.

Bristol 171 Sycamore 24 July 1947

The Bristol 171 Sycamore was the first British-designed helicopter to fly operationally and could accommodate five people – two at the front and three in the rear. The Sycamore carried out a number of military roles including casualty evacuation and air-sea rescue and was operated by BEA and the British and German armed services. It was in production from 1947-1959 and 175 were built of which 65 were exported.

Fairey Gyrodyne   7 December 1947

The Fairey Gyrodyne was a four/five-seater helicopter with a central rotor and a propeller on the right side only. It first flew in December 1947 and showed such promise that it set a speed record of 124 mph in June 1948. The first prototype, G-IKF, crashed in April 1949 by which time the second, G-AJJP (illustrated here), had flown but was converted to be the Jet Gyrodyne (see page 209).

Westland-Sikorsky WS.51 Dragonfly
5 October 1948

Having made the strategic decision to move into helicopter manufacture, Westland made an agreement with Sikorsky to licence-build its S-51 as the Westland-Sikorsky WS.51 Dragonfly with a British engine. The pilot was positioned centrally at the front with three passengers behind. Customers included the Royal Navy, RAF and many other armed services and some were also employed in civil use. 137 were built, 41 exported.

Cierva W.14 Skeeter 1   10 October 1948

Only one Cierva W.14 Skeeter was built. Registered G-AJCJ it was statically demonstrated at the Farnborough Air Show in September and then first flew in October 1948. Unfortunately, it was beset by shortcomings. The major problem was that the engine cooling was inadequate for its task and it soon overheated, and the Skeeter 2 with a different engine took over from it.

Cierva Air Horse 8 December 1948

The Cierva Air Horse was the largest helicopter of its type when it first flew in December 1948. It was unique in having three rotors all rotating in the same direction. The Air Horse was devised as a transport for which its capacious fuselage had clam shell doors at the rear. Unfortunately, it crashed killing the crew in June 1950 and the second Air Horse never flew as the Government ended the project.

Cierva W.14 Skeeter 2 15 October 1949

The Cierva W.14 Skeeter 2 was a much improved version of the Skeeter 1 with a new engine and a radical redesign, especially to its tail boom. It was registered G-ALUF and flew in October 1949, but it had severe problems with ground resonance and eventually broke up on the ground in June 1950.

Bristol 173 3 January 1952

The Bristol 173 which flew in January 1952 was Britain's first twin-engined helicopter and first tandem-rotor helicopter. This design, which was more of a 'proof of concept' vehicle, eventually resulted in the Bristol Belvedere (see page 212) and had a very long and troublesome development involving five machines while problems were sorted out.

Westland WS.55 Whirlwind (Piston engine)
12 November 1952

Westland took out a licence to build the Sikorsky S-55 in 1950 and named the British example the Westland WS.55 Whirlwind. Westland bought an S-55 and the Royal Navy also bought 25 directly from Sikorsky. Subsequent Whirlwinds were constructed by Westland, initially with American engines and later generally with British Alvis Leonides engines. The final version of the Whirlwind (Mks. 9, 10 and 12 for the UK armed forces) had the piston engine replaced with the Bristol Siddeley Gnome turbine engine (see page 210). A number of civil operators used it (as seen here with BEA) and Bristow Helicopters' Series 1s were used for oil rig support.

Fairey Jet Gyrodyne   8 January 1954

The Fairey Jet Gyrodyne was a rebuild of the Gyrodyne G-AJJP re-registered as XJ759 to act as a testbed for the Fairey Rotodyne. A much larger, tip-jet-driven rotor was fitted and as this had no torque it was possible to install pusher propellers on both stub wings. It flew in January 1954 and following trials was withdrawn from use. It is preserved at the Berkshire Museum of Aviation.

Fairey Ultra–Light Helicopter
14 August 1955

The Fairey Ultra-Light Helicopter lived up to its name: it was a two-seat observation helicopter with a two-bladed tip-jet-driven rotor of which six were built. It first flew in August 1955 and its various demonstrations were impressive. Though a technical success, it failed to break into either the British or US market and after four years of development, but no orders, the project came to an end.

Westland Widgeon 23 August 1955

Westland Aircraft decided to take advantage of the Dragonfly's capabilities by increasing the cabin capacity to carry five and using the rotor head, blades and gearbox from the Westland Whirlwind. Three Dragonflies were converted to WS-51 Series 2 Widgeons, and the first one flew in 1955. However the Widgeon was not a great success as only 12 more were built.

Westland Wessex (Sikorsky S-58)
17 May 1957

The Westland Wessex was built for the Royal Navy for anti-submarine warfare after it had decided that a development of the Bristol Belvedere would not suit the job. Westland purchased a Sikorsky S-58 (seen here) and speedily re-engined it with a Napier Gazelle turbine engine. This suited the Royal Navy which placed an order.

Fairey Rotodyne 6 November 1957

The Fairey Rotodyne was the world's first VTOL airliner. The Rotodyne was remarkably innovative; it could take off vertically from a city centre, transfer power to the propellers and cruise at approximately 175 mph to another city. The prototype XE521 flew in December 1957 – a bright future was expected but sadly the Rotodyne was overtaken by events and noise issues and in February 1962 the government cancelled the project.

Westland Westminster 15 June 1958

LEFT: The Westland Westminster grew from proposals for a 40-seater to fulfil a BEA requirement and for a flying crane. Westland constructed a flying test rig, G-APLE, (seen here) which flew in June 1958, joined by a second in 1959. In June 1960 G-APLE took to the air with its space frame structure given the appearance of a passenger-carrying helicopter (seen here). But there were insufficient funds so the project was cancelled in September 1960.

BELOW: The Westland Wessex entered service with the Navy on anti-submarine duties in 1961. Westland developed it further by installing twin Bristol Siddeley Gnome engines and the other services soon recognised its potential. So the RAF and Royal Marines bought the Wessex as a general-purpose helicopter capable of troop-carrying, air ambulance and ground support roles. A total of 356 were built.

Westland Wessex (UK build) 20 June 1958

Bristol 192 Belvedere 5 July 1958

TOP: The Bristol 192 Belvedere, the final development of the Bristol 173, flew in July 1958 eventually entering service with the RAF as a transport in September 1961. The Belvedere's performance was let down by engine problems and it was withdrawn from service in March 1969. There were two prototypes and 24 were delivered to the RAF.

MIDDLE: In 1956 work started on a small helicopter which became the Saunders-Roe P531. The first of two prototypes (seen here) flew in July 1958. The Army and Navy indicated definite interest in a larger version and Saunders-Roe carried out a substantial redesign, which became the P531-2 and P531-0 for the Army and the Royal Navy respectively and which led to their ordering the Westland Scout and Wasp.

BELOW: The final versions of the Westland Whirlwind received the Bristol Siddeley Gnome, a turbine engine which was not without its problems. The Royal Navy, RAF, Queen's Flight and Bristow Helicopters operated Gnome-powered Whirlwinds. The Whirlwind illustrated was the company demonstrator and had eight airline seats fitted. Total production of the Westland Whirlwind (all marks) was 418 with 90 exported.

Saunders-Roe P531 20 July 1958

Westland Whirlwind (Gnome engine) 28 February 1959

Westland Scout 4 August 1960

Wallis Autogiro 2 August 1961

Servotec Grasshopper 1 11 March 1962

TOP: The British Army was impressed by the redesign of the P531 and ordered a large number. Owing to production difficulties, entry into service was delayed and eventually the Scout only became operational in 1963. The Scout could accommodate 5/6 and could be used for casualty evacuation, command and control, reconnaissance and attack. It served all over the world with the Army, most notably in the Falklands. 148 were built.

MIDDLE: The Wallis Autogiro was developed by Wing Commander Ken Wallis who flew his first autogyro, the Wallis WA-116 Agile G-ARRT (seen here), in August 1961. After building ten single-seaters, construction of a two-seat variant, the WA-116T, was begun in 1969; he then tested a four-blade rotor and finally produced the WA-116F with which he won the closed-circuit world record in 1974.

BELOW: The Servotec Grasshopper 1 was a two-seat helicopter with a cabin reminiscent of a sports car. It was powered by a pair of piston engines mounted in the nose, which drove a pair of rotors mounted on a pylon just ahead of the cockpit. G-ARVN, the prototype (seen here), flew in March 1962, but was withdrawn from use in 1963 and scrapped in 1967.

Westland Wasp 28 October 1962

LEFT: *Following trials with the Saunders-Roe P531 the Royal Navy ordered the Sea Scout which was later renamed as the Westland Wasp. The Wasp shared the same design as the Army's Scout but had a folding tail boom and four-wheeled undercarriage. The Wasp could operate from warships to attack targets with torpedoes or missiles. Total production was 133 of which 35 were exported.*

BELOW: *In seeking a replacement for the Skeeter, the Army decided on the Bell 47G Sioux two-seater – a well-established design. In order to get quick delivery, the first 50 were built by Agusta in Italy and the remaining 100 by Westland. Subsequently the Army ordered another 116 and the RAF had 15, while the South Yemen Air Force received six and Bristow Helicopters, six. Total UK production amounted to 253.*

Westland Sioux 9 March 1965

Westland/Aerospatiale SA330 Puma HC1

15 April 1965

The RAF ordered 48 of these twin-engined medium-lift transport aircraft of which some 15 were produced by Westland, entering service in 1971. The total in service has been augmented by the purchase of a number of ex-SAAF aircraft all of which had much up-graded equipment fits. The MoD has recently placed a contract for the up-grade of the majority of those still in service, replacing the Turmo engines with the much more powerful Makila and augmenting the defensive aids suites.

Westland Aerospatiale SA341 Gazelle (France) 7 April 1967

The Gazelle was designed and first flown in France as a replacement for the Alouette II series. Originally known as the Sud Aviation SA341, the first aircraft (F-WOFH) was flown with a conventional three-bladed tail rotor from an Alouette II. The second prototype (F-ZWRA), and all subsequent production aircraft, were built with the now-familiar fenestron rotor, enclosed in a vertical fin. In May 1965 the British and French governments signed a Memorandum of Understanding for the design and production of three helicopters for the armed forces. The smallest of these was the SA341 Gazelle. The first British-built airframe (XW842) flew first on 31 January 1972 (see page 215).

Cierva CR-LTH Grasshopper Mk. 3

2 March 1969

The Cierva CR-LTH Grasshopper Mk. 3 followed the work done in developing the Servotec Grasshopper. Built in 1969 at Redhill in Surrey as an experimental five-seat helicopter, it was powered by two Rolls-Royce Continental piston engines. G-AWRP was the first of three to fly in June 1970 and proved a technical success but development was brought to an end owing to a lack of finance.

Westland Sea King 7 May 1969

Westland signed another agreement with Sikorsky in 1959 which led to a 1966 order by the Royal Navy for an anti-submarine warfare helicopter to replace the Wessex. The first Westland-built aircraft was delivered to the Navy in 1969 and amongst the many variants there was the Airborne Early Warning version (seen here). The Sea King proved very successful serving with the RAF and many other services. 344 were built.

Campbell Cricket Autogiro
November 1969

The Campbell Aircraft Company was founded in the late 1950s to develop and build autogyros and in 1969 began production of the single-seat Cricket at its factory in Membury. The Cricket design underwent a programme of continuous improvement under the auspices of its original designer Peter Lovegrove, who approved several additional features to make it more suitable for kit construction.

Westland WG13 Lynx 21 March 1971

The third helicopter covered by the 1965 Anglo-French Memorandum of Understanding was the Lynx, powered by twin Bristol-Siddeley Gem engines. It made its first flight on 21 March 1971. In 1972 the utility version took the helicopter speed record to just short of 200mph. It finally entered service as the Army's AH1 in 1976. In August 1986 the fully developed version with Gem 60 engines and BERP rotor took the world helicopter speed record to almost 250mph – a record that still stands. The latest version is the up-graded AH9 with LHTech T800 engines replacing the Gems.

Westland Gazelle (UK) 31 January 1972

A light, single-engined five-seat observation helicopter, the Gazelle was powered by a single Turbomeca Astanzou gas turbine. Production began in April 1970, with the delivery of the last of 262 aircraft in 1984. The Army took 197, the RN 31 and the RAF 34. Some 25 were delivered to civilian operators.

Westland Lynx (Navy) 25 May 1972

The first Navy Lynx flew in 1972 and entered service later that year. The Lynx is used for many roles including attack and armed with missiles such as the Sea Skua. It was heavily involved in the recent Iraq conflict. Lynxes have also been sold to seven navies including those of France and Brazil (seen here).

Campbell Cougar Autogiro 25 April 1973

The Campbell Cougar Autogiro is the sole example of a single-seater constructed by Western Airways at Weston-super-Mare Airport in early 1973. Powered by a single Rolls-Royce Continental piston engine, it first flew in April 1973 and is now preserved at the Helicopter Museum in Weston.

Westland-Sikorsky WS61 Sea King HC4
12 September 1973

The Westland Commando Mk. 1 was designed as a commando aircraft with simplified fixed undercarriage and non-folding rotor, although the HC4 version ordered by the RN retained the blade-folding facility.

Westland WG30   10 April 1979

During the early 1970s Westland's project office studied a possible civil version of the Lynx, which could take up to 19 passengers in VIP, passenger and cargo transport, and off-shore support roles. Design work began in 1977 on the WG30 which flew in 1979, but it proved only moderately successful. Westland produced 40 WG30s between 1978 and 1986.

Westland Lynx 3   14 June 1984

The Westland Lynx 3 was an enhanced variant with Westland 30 tail boom and rotor, Gem 60 engines, a new undercarriage and improved electronics. It was the result of a joint Westland/VFW-Fokker study for a combat helicopter for the French and German forces. However, the project did not materialise and only one prototype was built, ZE477 in 1984. Lynx development continues today with the AgustaWestland AW159 Lynx Wildcat.

Westland WS.70 1 April 1970

The manufacture of the Westland WS.70, capable of transporting two crew plus 20 troops, was a direct result of the association between Westland and Sikorsky, whereby Westland would build the Blackhawk under licence to supply to a Middle East customer. A single aircraft was built and flown, but events were overtaken by the outbreak of the Gulf War after which the requirement had changed.

AgustaWestland AW101 Merlin 7 October 1987

Developed as an Anglo-Italian project, the helicopter is a medium-lift three-engined machine with GE T800 engines for some variants, but with the higher-powered Rolls-Royce RTM322 in the UK versions. Designed as a Sea King replacement for the British and Italian armed forces, it first flew on 7 October 1987 and is now in service e with the RN, the RAF, the MMI, Portugal and the Canadian Armed Forces. A developed version designated VH71 has evolved for the US Presidential Flight. The Algerian Navy has recently placed a substantial order for this type.

Westland WAH 64D Apache 18 July 2000

The AH1D is a licence-built version of the Boeing AH-64D Apache Long-Bow attack helicopter with Rolls-Royce RTM322 engines replacing the US Army version's GE T-700. It has an augmented defensive aids suite and facility for folding rotor blades for ship-board use. A total of 67 has been delivered to the British Army.

Appendices

1 Airships and dirigibles

Bournemouth
Non-rigid built by Airship Club (Lord Ventry), 1951.
Data: 45,000 cu ft; length 108 ft; diameter 27 ft; height 45 ft; engine 1 x Salmson 60 hp; max speed 27 mph. Inflated with hydrogen. It made only eight flights.

Chitty Chitty Bang Bang
Semi-rigid Lebaudy replica made and flown for the film by Malcolm Brighton, 1967.
Data: 37,000 cu ft; diameter 30 ft; height 44 ft; engine 1 x VW 40 hp. First British airship to be inflated with helium.

Gloster
Non-rigid, designed by Harold Wingham and Bill Mays as an archaeological research platform but never completed, 1974.
Data: 25,000 cu ft; length 82 ft; diameter 25 ft; engines 2 x Hirth F10-A18 26 hp.

Santos Dumont
Non-rigid built by Anthony Smith, 1974.
Data: 33,000 cu ft length 76 ft; diameter 29 ft; engines 2 x Wankel 20 hp; max speed 30 mph. First inflated with hydrogen, later helium.

AD 500-01
Non-rigid built by Aerospace Developments (designed by Roger Munk), 1976.
Only flew twice on 3 February and 8 March 1979 and destroyed in storm 9 March 1979. Data: 182,000 cu ft; length 170.5 ft; diameter 48.7 ft; engines 2 x Porsche 930 inboard engines with outboard ducted propellors. Prototype of Skyship 500 series and later became known as Skyship 500-01.

Skyship 500-02
First true Skyship. First flew 28 September 1981 with upgraded, turbo-charged, 206 hp engines.

Skyship 500HL
(HL = Heavy Lift) Skyship 500 gondola with the larger SK 600 envelope. The first, SK500-04, first flew March 1984. In all six SK 500 and SK 500 HL models were built and flown and some of the 500s were later converted to 500HLs.

Skyship 600 series
Larger version of SK 500 non-rigid series built by Airship Industries (Roger Munk). First flew March 1984. Nine were built and some still operate with Airship Management Services in the USA.
Data: 210,000 cu ft (later 247,500 cu ft); length 197 ft; diameter 51 ft; engines 2 x Porsche 930/67, 300 hp engines, similar to AD 500 but bigger. Later extended as SKS-600B. One was later fitted with Textron Lycoming 10-510, 300 hp, turbine engines outboard driving the swivelling ducted propellors and first flew 18 January 2002.

AT-10
Non-rigid built by Airship Technology Group (designed by Roger Munk), 2003 .
Data: 88,287 cu ft; length 136 ft; diameter 35 ft; engines 2 x Diesel Air 100 hp outboard in front of ducted propellors. First flew 28 March 2002. Exported to China.

Cameron Balloons and its subsidiary Thunder and Colt (T&C) manufacture both helium and hot air airships.

Don Cameron designed and built the world's first hot air airship, the D-96, which first flew on 4 January 1973. Length 100 ft., dia 46 ft, height 60 ft, engine VW 40 hp.

Cameron's first helium airship, DG-19, flew in 1983. T&C was the first company to build a pressurised hot air airship. The designs available in 2009 are:
AS-80 Mk. II (80,000 cu ft)
AS-105 Mk. II (105,000 cu ft)
AS-120 Mk. II (120,000 cu ft)

AS-80 GD and AS-105 GD have been further developed by GEFA-FLUG in Germany.

Thunder and Colt developed the largest hot air airship in the world, the AS-261, to drop an observation platform in the canopy of tropical rainforests. In 1993 the ship was fitted with a larger replacement envelope manufactured by Lindstrand Balloons and has since been known as the AS-300 (300,000 cu ft). T&C also produced and type-certified the GA-42 non-rigid helium airship, capable of carrying two persons. Six GA-42 airships were built. Two were reported to be originally flying in Shanghai but believed to have crashed, and there are two for sale, one being in the USA. The rights to the GA-42 design were acquired by the American Blimp Corporation when T&C was acquired by Cameron Balloons Ltd in 1995.

Lindstrand has the two firms of Lindstrand Balloons and Lindstrand Technologies.

Lindstrand Balloons manufactures the HS110 hot air or thermal airship (110,000 cu ft).

Lindstrand Technologies (LT) built the GA-22 unmanned airship (22,000 cu ft) one of which was purchased by the Spanish Ministry of Defence. LT has now also built and is testing GA-22 Mk. II (14,000 cu ft) in conjunction with BAe Systems.

2 Home-built and replicas

The following list of aircraft have all been built and flown in the UK since the end of the war. They have all been built in relatively small numbers – indeed many of them are unique, one-off production efforts, entirely designed and constructed by an active 'home-building' community. Others have been assembled from professionally prepared plans, and/or from complete kits of ready-to-assemble parts. Some of these kits have been prepared by overseas manufacturers to their own designs, but in each case the individual aircraft listed here are the first of their type to be completed and flown in the UK – in many cases, other examples of the same design have subsequently been built by additional owners. The list also includes a large number of replica aircraft – often built for film work, but occasionally for display-flying by an individual owner. Certain aircraft have been omitted from this list because their designs have gone on to become commercially successful in their own right: in such cases, the entry will be found in the main listing.

Finding accurate first-flight dates is a horribly inexact science in this particular field of research. Many dates are almost unknown, while others are both vague and variable, depending on the original source material. I have tried to consult widely separate sources to confirm the dates shown below, but I still find it impossible to guarantee their accuracy.

Helmy Aerogypt IV (G-AFFG)
17 February 1946

Wren Goldcrest (G-AICX) 1947

Heath Parasol (G-AFZE) 9 January 1949

Britten-Norman Druine Turbi (G-APFA) 13 May 1957

Bellamy Currie Wot (G-APNT)
11 September 1958

P.P.S. Vickers 22 'Replica' (Anon) 1960

Thurston Tawney Owl (G-APWU)
22 April 1960

P.P.S. Demoiselle Replica (Anon) 1963

Miles Bristol Boxkite Replica (Anon)
April 1964

Hants Aero Club Avro Triplane Replica (Anon) 9 May 1964

Eardley-Billing Replica (Anon)
14 June 1964

Miles SE5A Replica (G-ATGV) 1965

P.P.S. Pfalz D.III Replica (G-ATIF / EI-ARD) 1965

P.P.S. Fokker E.III Replica (G-AVJO / 157) April 1965

VAFA Vickers FB.5 Gunbus Replica (G-ATVP) 14 June 1966

Brooklands Mosquito (G-ATSW) July 1966

Bellamy Avro 504K Replica (G-ATXL) 17 August 1966

Jurca MJ-2 Tempete (G-ASUS) 2 October 1966

Gowland Jenny Wren (G-ASRF) 13 October 1966

Slingsby T.56 (SE.5A Replica) (G-AVOT) 20 June 1967

Ward Gnome (G-AXEI) 4 August 1967

Jodel D.9 Bebe (G-AWFT) 1968

Gardan Minicab (G-AVRW) 1968

Slingsby Capstan (G-AWDV) 15 February 1968

Storey TSR.3 Wonderplane (G-AWIV) 25 July 1968

Jodel D.11 (G-AWMD) 1969

Airmark/Cassutt IIIM racer (G-AXDZ) 1969

P.P.S. Morane Type N Replica (G-AWBU) 1969

Slingsby T.57 Camel Replica (G-AWYY) 4 March 1969

Slingsby Rumpler C. IV Replica (G-AXAL) 24 March 1969

VAFA Vickers FB.27 Vimy Replica (G-AWAU) 3 June 1969

Owl Racer (G-AYMS) early 1971

Falconar (Jodel) F.9 (G-AYEG) 1971

Shield Xyla (G-AWPN) 30 October 1971

Mignet HM.293 (G-AXPG) 1972

AJEP Tailwind (G-AYDU) 24 March 1972

Evans VP-1 (G-AYXW) 29 June 1972

Airmaster H2-B1 helicopter (G-AYNS) 12 September 1972

Volmer Sportsman (G-BAHP) 1973

Crosby BA-4B (G-AYFU) 25 March 1973

Pitts Special S.1C (G-AXNZ) 6 June 1973

Phoenix PM.3 Duet (G-AYTT) 22 June 1973

St Cyrien Sopwith Pup Replica (G-APUP) 11 August 1973

Coates SA.2 Swalesong (G-AYDV) 10 September 1973

Bushby Midget Mustang (G-AWIR) 14 October 1973

P.P.S. Manning-Flanders 'Replica' (Anon) 1 March 1974

Jurca MJ-5 Sirocco (G-AZOS) 21 June 1974

Isaacs Spitfire (G-BBJI) 5 May 1975

Leisure Sport S.5 Replica (G-BDFF) 28 August 1975

K & S SA-102 Cavalier (G-AZHH) 6 December 1975

IES Vickers FB.5 Gunbus Replica (ZS-JHN) June 1976

Whittaker MW.2 Excalibur (G-BDDX) 1 July 1976

Bellamy Fokker DR.1 Replica (G-BEFR) December 1976

DAW Privateer Srs.2 (G-BCYH) late 1976

Bellamy Sopwith Camel Replica (G-BFCZ) 1977

Falconar (Jodel) F.11 (G-BDPL) 1977

Great Lakes Baby (G-BBGL) June 1977

Jurca MJ-7 Gnatsum (G-BEFU) 5 October 1977

Bede BD-4E (G-BEKL) 7 October 1977

Brugger MB.2 Colibri (G-BFBV) late 1977

Plumb BGP-1 (G-BGPI) circa 1978

Wallis 'Wallbro' Monoplane Replica (G-BFIP) 10 August 1978

Bellamy DH.2 Replica (G-BFVH) mid 1978

Turner Super Wot (G-BEPO) June 1979

Western A/c Flycatcher Replica (G-BEYB / S1287) July 1979

Western A/c Sopwith Replica (G-BIDW / 9382) November 1980

Szep HFC125 (G-BCPX) circa 1980

Kendal Mayfly (G-PFAK) June 1981

Ward E.47 Elf (G-MMUL) 7 April 1984

Noble Hardman Snowbird (G-MNHA) 2 September 1984

Western A/c Hawker Fury Replica (G-BKBB) 11 December 1985

Sopwith Pup Replica (G-BIAT) 2 July 1986

Sopwith Triplane Replica (G-PENY) late 1988

Bonsall Mustang (G-BDWA) 1991

Sopwith Triplane Replica (G-BOCK) 10 April 1992

Sherwood Ranger (G-MWND) October 1992

Sopwith Dove Replica (G-EAGA) 28 March 1993

A.J.D./E.T.S. Avro 504K Replica (G-ECKE) 29 September 1994

Acro Advanced (G-BPAA) October 1994

Lynn Williams Z.1 Flitzer (G-BVAW/ D692) April 1995

Sopwith Triplane Replica (G-BWRA /N500) August 1996

Cliff Piper Metisse (G-BVCP) 19 December 1999

Bristol M.1C Monoplane Replica (G-BWJM) 25 September 2000

Lynden Aurora (G-CBZS) 11 October 2003

3 Gliders and sailplanes

This is not intended to be a comprehensive list, but includes most gliders and sailplanes designed and/or built in the UK since January 1945. A few replicas of pre-1945 or foreign types and most projected types that did not fly have been deliberately excluded, apart from a few "one offs" that may have been inadvertently omitted.

1945 **Armstrong Whitworth A.W. 52G** Two-seat experimental research glider. Conventional construction but covered in "Plymax" material (ply and light alloy sheet).

1945 **Slingsby Type 23 Kite 1A** Single-seat sailplane, a post-war development of the Type 6 Kite 1.

1945 **The Colditz Cock** Open two-seater glider. 32 ft span. Designed and built by British prisoners of war in Colditz Castle, Germany, to effect an escape. Never flew. A replica flew in 2000.

1945 **Chilton Olympia** Built by Chilton Aircraft Ltd. British version of German D.F.S. 70 Olympia-Meise. Single-seat sailplane of conventional wooden construction. Production taken over by Elliotts of Newbury.

1946 **Slingsby Type 24 Falcon 4** Two-seat tandem seating sailplane of conventional wooden construction. Designed by Slingsby

Sailplanes Ltd and built by Martin Hearn Ltd.

1946 Short Nimbus Two-seat tandem high performance sailplane designed by A.O. Mattocks & built by members of Short Bros Gliding Club in aircraft works at Rochester, Kent. Of conventional wooden construction. Only one built.

1947 EON Type 5 Olympia 1 Single-seat sailplane of conventional wooden construction. Elliotts improved and developed version of Chilton Olympia. Olympia 1 had main skid only, Olympia 2 was fitted with a fixed central wheel and Olympia 3 had skid complete with dolly wheels.

1947 Hawkridge Venture Two-seat side-by-side sailplane of conventional wooden construction, designed & built by Hawkridge Aircraft Ltd of Dunstable.

1947 De Havilland Horsa II with Comet nose Research glider. 88ft. span.

1947 Martin Dagling Training glider. 33ft. span.

1948 Slingsby Type 25 Gull 4 Single-seat 50ft. sailplane designed by Slingsby Sailplanes as replacement for D.F.S. Meise Olympia. Conventional wooden construction.

1948 Slingsby Type 26 Kite 2 Single-seat medium performance sailplane, developed from Type 23 Kite 1A and Type 23A. Prototype built by Slingsby, but production examples built by Martin Hearn Ltd.

1948 Slingsby Type 30 Prefect Single-seat intermediate sailplane, an improved and developed version of Type 5 Grunau Baby.

1948 EON Type 7 S.G. 38 Primary Single-seat primary glider of wooden construction. Elliots version of German-designed D.F.S. 14 S.G. 38 Primary glider.

1948 EON Type 8 Baby Eon Single-seat sailplane of conventional wooden construction. Elliotts improved version of German-designed D.F.S 49 Grunau Baby 2b. Elliotts version had enclosed canopy.

1948 Broburn Sailplane Wanderlust Small training glider. 34ft. span.

1949 Hawkridge Kittiwake A repaired, rebuilt and modified Slingsby T.15 Gull 3. Also known as the Cantilever Gull.

1949 Gardner Cumulus Single-seat light-wing sailplane. Conventional wooden construction, but very lightly built. Wrecked on first test flight at Dunstable.

1949 Nyborg TGN 3 Type of flying wing research glider. Flew at Stratford. 34.5ft. span.

1950 Slingsby Type 31 Tandem Tutor Two-seat tandem glider for initial stages of glider flying. Conventional wooden construction.

1950 Slingsby Type 34A Sky 1 Single-seat high-performance sailplane. 18 m version of Type 25 Gull 4. Wings and fuselage both lengthened. Philip Wills won the 1952 World Championships in Spain in a Sky.

1951 Short S.B.1 Single-seat experimental glider built by Short Bros and Harland at Belfast to test aerodynamic properties of the aeroisoclinic wing developed by Professor G.T.R. Hill and D. Keith-Lucas. Only one built. It crashed and was wrecked on its fourth flight.

1952 Slingsby Type 38 Grasshopper TX. Mk. 1 Single-seat primary glider designed for use of the Air Training Corps and School Squadrons by the Combined Cadet Forces. Fuselage was a simplified version of the German S.G. 38 primary glider, to which the wings and modified tail unit of the Type 7 Cadet Mk. 1 glider were fitted.

1953 Davis-Costin Condor Two-seat tandem sailplane of conventional wooden construction. Only one built.

1953 Slingsby Type 37 Skylark 1 Single-seat experimental sailplane. Fuselage based on Type 30 Prefect fuselage.

1953 Slingsby Type 41 Skylark 2 Single-seat sailplane, originally known as Type 37B. A developed version of Skylark 1, with extended wingspan, decreased wing loading and ply monocoque fuselage. Of conventional wooden construction.

1954 Kendall Crabpot & K.1 Initial version was Crabpot designed by H. Kendall for the 1947 B.G.A. two-seat sailplane competition. Project only. It was redesigned, wing being manufactured by F.G. Miles at Redhill as Miles M.76, but, when tested, it broke up. The K.1, as the Crabpot was then known, was later built, using traditional wooden construction methods, by Elliotts of Newbury, as EON Type 9. Only one built. First flight at Lasham in March 1954. Abandoned owing to unsolvable spinning problems.

1954 Slingsby Type 42 Eagle Two-seat tandem sailplane of wooden construction, originally designed to meet possible A.T.C. requirements for a high-performance two-seat training sailplane

1954 EON Type 5 Olympia 4 Developed version of Olympia 1 with redesigned wing. Olympia 401 was revised version of Olympia 4, while Olympia 402 was converted Olympia 4 prototype converted to 55.75ft. span for 1956 World Championships.

1955 Slingsby Type 43 Skylark 3 Single-seat competition sailplane. Enlarged and developed version of Skylark 2, with

increased span and higher aspect ratio. Of conventional wooden construction, with Gaboon ply covering.

1957 EON Type 6 Olympia 403 Single-seat sailplane of wooden construction, developed from Olympia 401 and 402. The 55.75ft. wing of the 402 was fitted to a similar fuselage to the 401 but with increased nose length, strengthened and shortened rear fuselage. Revised fin and rudder with all-moving tailplane.

1957 Slingsby Type 46 Two-seat side-by-side glider, a developed version of Type 21B with larger wingspan, enclosed cockpit and revised tail unit. Also known as Slingsby T.21C.

1958 Reussner Swift Started life as the prototype Slingsby T.45 in 1957. Modifications included extending wingspan to 49.25ft., lengthening fuselage by one foot. Revised canopy was fitted.

1958 Shenstone Harbinger Two-seat tandem sailplane designed by B.S. Shenstone and W. Czerwinski for the 1947 two-seat sailplane design competition. Of conventional wooden construction apart from a metal main frame in the fuselage, and a metal tripod in the wing. One built by F. Coleman of Great Hucklow, Derbyshire and another in Canada.

1958 EON Type 6 Olympia 419 Single-seat sailplane, developed from Olympia 403. Revised fuselage with all-moving, folding tailplanes.

1959 Westmacott Skylark Single-seat biplane glider designed and built by two bothers, R. J. and K. Westmacott at Minety near Malmesbury, Wiltshire. Only one built.

1960 EON Type 10 EON 460 Single-seat standard class sailplane, of wooden construction.

1961 Breeze Oozle Bird Training glider. Nothing known.

1961 EON Type 6 Olympia 419 Single-seat sailplane, developed from Olympia 403. Revised fuselage with all-moving, folding, tailplanes. Olympia 415 was Standard Class version of 419, with reduced wingspan.

1960 Davis-Costin Condor 2 Rebuilt Condor with longer nose and other detail alterations. Crashed and written off 1961.

1961 Slingsby Type 50 Skylark 4 Single-seat sailplane. Final development of T.43 Skylark 3. Fuselage was restyled. Larger canopy fitted.

1961 Slingsby Type 49 Capstan Side-by-side Two-seat sailplane suitable for all stages of dual training. Of conventional wooden construction, with Gaboon ply covering, with nose section and other double-curvature panels and fairings being made of glass fibre reinforced plastic.

1963 **Slingsby Type 51 Dart** Single-seat high-performance sailplane, of construction as of Type 49. Wing spars were initially all wood but were later of mixed wood and metal light alloy. Dart 15 had 49.25ft. wingspan and Dart 17, 55.75ft.

1963 **EON Type 10 EON 460/463** Production versions of Eon 460.

1963 **Peak 100** High-performance side-by-side two-seat sailplane designed by Bedford Sailplane Design Group and built by Peak Sailplanes in Derbyshire. Wings and tail unit of conventional spruce and ply construction while fuselage was of steel tubular welded construction, fabric covered. All-moving tailplane. Only one built.

1965 **EON Type 10 EON 465** Development of Eon 460/463 designed for 1965 World Championships.

1966 **Chard Osprey** Single-seat Standard Class sailplane of conventional wooden construction. Only one built. Based on Slingsby Dart 15 fitted with entirely new wing, designed by Keith Chard and built at Lasham.

1967 **Slingsby/Schreder HP-14** Single-seat high-performance sailplane, built under licence from Bryan Aircraft of Ohio, USA, by Slingsby Sailplanes Ltd. All metal light alloy construction, with 'V' tailplane.

1967 **Slingsby Type 53** two-seat high-performance sailplane of all metal light alloy construction. The T53A was prototype and had tapered wing fitted with flaps. Type 53B was production version. Redesigned simplified structure, flaps deleted. Conventional tailplane and elevators in place of all-moving type tailplane. Cockpit moved forward. Type 53C had revised and extended fin and rudder, no dorsal fin. A.T.C. version.

1968 **Slingsby HP-14C** Single-seat high-performance sailplane. A development by Slingsby Sailplanes Ltd of the original Schreder design. Wingspan increased to 59ft., conventional tail unit. All metal light alloy construction.

1968 **Slingsby T.49C Powered Capstan** Standard Capstan two-seat sailplane fitted with 45hp. Nelson H-63CP engine mounted on pylon above the wings, driving a pusher propeller.

1969 **Ginn-Lesniak Kestrel** Two-seat tandem semi-aerobatic sailplane. Only one built, at Dunstable.

1970 **Birmingham Guild Moore Gypsy** Single-seat small sailplane designed by L.P. Moore, J. Gibson and K. Emslie in 1965.

Fuselage of metal monoque construction with G.R.P. nose. First flight 1970.

1970 **Slingsby Type 59 Glasflugel Kestrel** Single-seat high-performance sailplane, built under licence from Glasflugel, of Schlattstall, near Stuttgart, Germany. G.R.P construction. 55.75ft. version and 62.3ft. versions known as T.59C and T.59D. The 72.2ft. version is T.59H.

1970 **Slingsby T.61 Falke** Licence-built version of Scheibe SF-25B two-seat side-by-side powered low-wing sailplane, intended mainly for training. Fabric-covered welded steel-tube structure. Wings of wooden cantilever construction.

1971 **Operation Sigma, Sigma 1 Type C** Modification at Cranfield of Types A & B destroyed in Slingsby fire. Single-seat high-performance competition sailplane. Of mixed, but mainly all metal light alloy, construction.

1971 **Torva 15 Sprite and Sprint** Single-seat sailplane for training and recreational use (Sprite) and recreational and competition flying (Sprint). G.R.P construction.

1971 **Holmes KH-1** Single-seat high-performance homebuilt sailplane, designed and built by Kenneth Holmes. Conventional all-wood semi-monocoque structure.

1972 **Birmingham Guild BG Gypsy 135** Single-seat low-cost lightweight production development of Birmingham Guild Moore Gypsy (BG100/12) prototype.

1972 **Manuel Hawk** Single-seat amateur sailplane, designed for soaring in weak thermal conditions. Designed by W.L. Manuel, built at Fairoaks and modified structurally at Cranfield under direction of Howard A. Torode. Conventional all-wood semi-monocoque structure.

1973 **Yorkshire Sailplanes YS53 Sovereign** Tandem two-seat training sailplane. Modified version of Slingsby T.53B by Yorkshire Sailplanes which had acquired rights to this aircraft. Light alloy semi-monocoque structure.

1973 **Yorkshire Sailplanes YS 55 Consort** Production version of BG Gypsy 135 developed by Birmingham Guild from which Yorkshire Sailplanes acquired manufacturing rights in 1973.

1974 **1853 Cayley Flyer replica** Designed by Cdr. John Sproule and built by Ken Fripp and co-workers of Southdown Aero Services at Lasham. Span 23ft. Flown by Derek Piggott in 1986.

1975 **Swales SD3-15T and SD-15V** Single-seat sailplanes. V and T respectively denote tail configuration. Semi-monocoque

structure of four longerons, metal stressed skin and G.R.P nosecone.

1976 **Manuel Condor** Training two-seat glider. 50.2ft. span.

1977 **Halford JHS Scorpion** Open class. 18 m span.

1977 **Slingsby T.61F Venture** Special version of Slingsby T.61 Falke, ordered by Ministry of Defence for Air Training Corps, known by RAF as Venture T. Mk. 2. T.61G is civil development varying mainly in having different propulsion unit.

1977 **Vickers-Slingsby Vega** Single-seat high-performance 49.2ft. Standard Class sailplane. Conventional semi-monocoque structure, mostly G.R.P.

1979 **Wright Falcon 15 m** Single-seat homebuilt 15 m Class sailplane. Designed and built by Peter W. Wright. Cantilever mid-wing monoplane. Cantilever V tail surfaces. G.R.P. construction.

1984 **Lightwing Rooster** Single-seat slow speed research soaring biplane. Designed and built by John M. Lee. Unequal span biplane of wood construction with double surface fabric covering.

1984 **Lightwing L6FS Mouse** Single-seat lightweight research sailplane. Designed and built by Jon M. Lee. Wood construction. Fabric covered wings, fuselage and tail surfaces. Cantilever high-wing monoplane. with cruciform tail unit. Rectangular box fuselage.

1987 **Lightwing CT6 Companion** Tandem two-seat training glider. Designed and built by John M. Lee. Cantilever high-wing monoplane. G.R.P construction.

1993 **Lightwing (J Lee) Penrose Pegasus** Light glider. John Lee rebuild. 34.75ft. span.

1994 **Edgley EA-9 Optimist** High-performance glider. 49.2ft. span.

2000 **Colditz Cock Replica** Built by Southdown Aero Services, Lasham and flown by John Lee at RAF Odiham in the presence of about 14 of the veterans who had worked on the original at Colditz Castle in 1945.

2003 **1853 Cayley Flyer replica** Designed and built by RAeS Brough branch with financial backing of BAe Systems at Brough and Virgin Atlantic. Span 23ft. Flown by Allan McWhirter

Credits

Index